Copyright

MOOOVE AHEAD!

of the corporate herd

Tony Wong

* * *

ISBN: 978-1-300-26386-9

Mooove Ahead!

Of the Corporate Herd

By

Tony Wong

Contents

Twitter = Mooovers.

Facebook = Mooove Ahead

Website = Mooveahead.com

Email = moooveahead@yahoo.com

Prologue

With a daughter and several nephews and nieces who have graduated or are soon-to-graduate from college, the topic of how to find jobs came up often; what job or career to take; what to do when you get a job; what to expect in the office; what land mines to avoid; how to get ahead. After many similar conversations, I began recalling a number of things about working and succeeding in a corporate environment that I wish I had known when I was that age. I made notes of the experiences and tips and the result is this book, which I wished was available when I entered the corporate world. The sad truth is I did not even look for books or advice at that age. You know what the old adage: hindsight is 20/20.

The insights in this book are valuable even to "older", mid-career people currently working in corporations. It was amazing to me how many people (including myself) in their 30's and 40's did not learn the things that are outlined in the pages that follow. When I was able to step back, I realized most people are so busy between work and family, they don't learn or notice how the corporate world really works and just don't know how to get ahead. And let's face it, there is the phenomenon about being "too close to the tree to see the whole forest" or in this case, those subtle things needed to get ahead in the corporate world.

Early on I realized that there were certain things that some people would never have the opportunity to even learn unless they held senior management positions, and that's the majority of the working population. The corporate world hierarchy is a pyramid with most of the herd working their entire career in the bottom half of the pyramid. For this reason, much of this book applies to any current employees in the corporate world who are below middle management, and not just the young newcomers. This book is a collection of what I've learned from many years working at public and private corporations, where I reached a Director position in several Fortune 125 organizations. In many ways, I feel I was very lucky to have reached an Executive level. The process for me was definitely hit or miss, largely based on the "school of hard knocks" with a large helping of luck. I had no parental advice (my parents were immigrants and never worked in a corporation). Growing up as a minority, there seemed to be a shortage of mentors especially among the corporate "ruling class" of Caucasian males or, perhaps, it was because I did not ask or try hard enough to seek them out.

In any case, I did not know how important getting advice and mentoring was. As the saying goes, "I didn't know what I didn't know".

That said, you can embark on a path of chance and luck like I did OR you can take the first step and do what I was never smart enough to do early in my career -- learn from others. I'm here to help you increase your advancement opportunities and learn these insights faster (unlike myself and many other "worker bees" who are well past the age of 30).

The quick advice:

1. Listen/inquire/seek advice from people with experience and success.

2. Be mindful of the advice and execute. Thinking about something and working on something is good, but they are only 5% of the success factor. Getting things across the finish line is 95%. Execute!

3. Keep going back to 1. It's not a one-time event. Seriously, the above commandments are absolutely true. But for the sake of the money you invested in this book, the least I can give you in return is more detailed advice on what I've learned, collected, and yes, that "R" word...researched.

With the help of other corporate "players", including people at various levels in an organization, various job roles, and even consultants to corporations (because they bring a very unique view of how corporations operate), the following is a collection of valuable wisdom, tips, and insights you will NEVER learn in college and, for some reason, is rarely shared by the herd of corporate employees who have come before you.

Go to any bookstore like Barnes & Noble or peruse online and look through the management sections for similar advice books. I've done this, of course, and sadly there are very few readily available books providing operational insight. "Operational" -- to mean advice from an *operating* manager about being successful in daily corporate life. Most books were about vision and strategy. They're great reading, but they are targeted to CEOs and General Managers. Some of you will get there, but to get there you have to be successful for the foreseeable years at the operating level. By my survey, 80% of the books are written by consultants, researchers, and university professors. Where are all the operating managers and their daily, real corporate world insight? The other 20% percent of the books are very practical and useful for getting into a herd...they're about finding a job and how to dress. Again, where are the books by operating managers about how to successfully get ahead of the herd?

I will discuss myths and realities, of course from my perspective, but I believe you will find they apply to all equally. And where an insight or situation applies differently because of gender, race, culture, or religion, I'll speak to it...because that's the real corporate world. Although I did not personally conduct extensive primary research, my perspective is based on first hand experiences as an Operating Manager/Director and my readings of secondary research others have published.

Throughout this book, I will also share many business sayings and idioms. They stuck with me throughout my career and life because they are useful, timeless tips. They don't teach them in school, but you may have heard some already. Many have crossed into the general culture. Here's one I alluded to at the start of this introduction and is perfectly apropos for this book, "I wish I knew then what I know now" ~ Unknown.

I heard Meg Whitman (x-CEO of eBay) use several adages (they're in this book) in a speech she gave during her 2010 run as the Republican candidate for Governor of California. One she used was, "Plan your work, then work your plan". This saying is so simple yet so profound. When I was first taught this habit, I thought it was a waste of time. I reluctantly followed the practice using a tool known as a DayTimer (it was essentially a small binder calendar and very popular in the late '80s). At some point, technologies such as calendar software on smartphones and personal computers made the manual DayTimer and similar products obsolete, but the practice of planning your work and working your plan continued. Before I knew it, I bought into the usefulness of the practice and it has become a normal habit in my life. The saying included in Whitman's speech has so many benefits that it is recognized and applied in many important areas of business and life. For example, every life coach demands that you write down your goals and then develop tactics to reach each goal. Isn't that just another way of saying, "Plan your work, and work your plan"? Every financial planner or advisor's first order of business with a client is to have the client write down their financial goals. A business plan is mostly an exercise in writing down the goals for the business and the tactics to achieve the goals. Corporate Strategic planning and the tactical targets used for operational reviews is another example. As an individual, you should plan your work down to a daily level if necessary, depending upon your position and responsibilities, then work your plan.

Chapter 0.9 – Congratulations, welcome to the herd!

"Don't reinvent the wheel" ~ Unknown

Time to mooove from the college herd to the corporate herd.

Why the cow metaphor? As I began writing this book and recalling my working days in the corporate world, I had a constant image of an incident I had at a movie theater when I was in my early twenties. My wife-to-be and I were waiting for the doors of the movie theater to open. It was a sold out movie and we were crammed in the lobby along with all the other moviegoers. At some point, one of the moviegoer blurred out, "mmmmooooooooooo". Quickly others joined in. The crowd sounded exactly what they felt like, a herd of cows. It was hilarious. A herd of cows is so symbolic of the typical employees in the corporate world. Cows are social animals. They pack in herds. Most are followers. Just as cows all have spots and appear to look alike, every employee looks like every other employee, but what's different is beneath the spots. Some become leaders and achievers. Which will you be? That depends on how you control those things you can control, starting with your formal education.

Congratulations to those of you who just graduated with a college degree. You are a college grad!! You should be proud of your achievement. Avoid the temptation of thinking that everyone has one; everyone does not. In the United States, less than 30% of the population have a bachelor's degree or higher. It's not easy. You would think that in our society, with public schooling and a relative ease of access to colleges, the number should be 60%+. Our country needs to move in that direction if it is to compete in the global labor market. Anyhow, sorry for digressing. You are one of the few that achieved it. Congratulations! It's a long road (16 years including kindergarten) and the cost of a 4 year degree (just the cost of the college portion) is anywhere from $12,000 to over $200,000 depending upon where you attended college(s). So, stand tall and appreciate your accomplishment.

If you're a mid-career individual contributor (not by choice), congratulations for your curiosity in improving your career. You probably thought, or have desired at this stage in your career, to be in a leadership role. Congratulations for asking yourself, "Why?" and "What can I do?" or better yet, "What didn't I do?" And congratulations for not blaming others for your career situation. At the end of the day, it is YOUR career and yours to control.

Congratulations to both groups reading this because you have shown a desire to learn from others (namely me, people I've learned from, people I've gathered wisdom from, and hopefully others you will latch onto who can provide you valuable insight that can help you to attain your professional and even personal goals).

In general, the mid-careerist's situation is vastly different than that of young people just entering the corporate workforce, but there is one very common shared item – you both lack the insight to efficiently AND effectively navigate the corporate environment.

Young people don't learn corporate career insights in their academic curriculum. Most parents don't pass on the information, if they know it at all. Few books are written to convey the information. And, unfortunately, many people work for years in the corporate world without learning the information for a variety of different reasons.

Aside from a scarcity of books on corporate insights, there is a dearth of corporate career insight among the masses of corporate workers. The number one reason may be with the individual. People do not seek out the advice. There is no shame, but people don't like to ask for help. "Don't reinvent the wheel" is a popular business saying. This is a simple concept that most people understand, but don't follow. Learning from others in order to avoid obstacles or to follow a faster, easier path is the lesson from that saying, but the majority of people (young or mid-career) don't do it. We won't go into the psycho-analysis of "why". Facts are facts, most people simply don't. The ones that figure it out or do it by accident mooove ahead sooner. Therefore, it's good to be a minority in this respect.

This book is primarily targeted to anyone trying to get a job in the corporate world OR anyone who has been working in the corporate world for 10 plus years and aspires but is:

A. Not a manager.

B. Just a first level manager/supervisor.

This fits probably 95% of you.

If you are already in a herd (cow speak for working in a corporation), skip to Chapter 4 "Brand You" and start there.

If you're in a herd but are in search of another herd, skip to Chapter 2 "Getting a Corporate Job".

The rest of you therefore must be "calves" looking to break into a herd, so start at the beginning, Chapter 1 "Begin at the Beginning". It's a proven fact that you have to start somewhere and I'll explain how to get started in the corporate world to position yourself to break away from the herd.

Find Your Starting Point

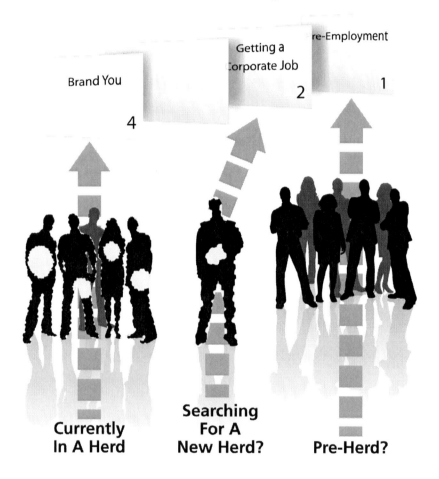

Chapter 1 – Begin at the Beginning, Pre-Employment (Pre-herd)

"Failure to prepare is preparing to fail" ~ Unknown

This book is about getting ahead in the corporate world, but the beginning really starts before you enter the corporate world. It starts with preparation: your formal and informal education, the formative experiences that have shaped you; the path you've chosen so far; the plan (if any) which you've followed to date, and lastly your goals.

If you want to get ahead of the herd, the work you do before you start your job can make a big difference in getting ahead of many members of the particular herd you choose to join. So what should or shouldn't you do? Let's explore some myths and realities.

Myth: College Doesn't Really Help

Maybe you believe that a college degree doesn't really matter. Maybe you believe there are better ways to spend your time. You may be right, there are many ways to spend the time you might otherwise spend in college.

Reality: College Helps if You Want to Get Ahead of the Herd

The reality is that college doesn't hurt. It is a learning opportunity and learning is what this book promotes. The opportunity cost of going to college is time. So if you are not going to spend your time getting a college education, do something productive with your time. There are many ways you can spend the time, but if you are planning to get ahead of the herd, college matters for a single, powerful reason – leadership executive positions almost always require a 4-year college degree. Remember, we're discussing the general rule and not that glorified "exception to the rule." However, I'll admit college is not the only way to find your career path. How to succeed by taking other paths is another book for another time.

Myth: The Type of College Doesn't Really Matter

When choosing a college, you may think that the type of college doesn't matter. Or you may wonder if the college you choose should be a four-year university.

Reality: If You Can Afford It, Go To The Best College

If you cannot afford a four-year university, I am a big fan (and there is lots of proof) of starting at a community college and then transferring to a four-year college. Some would argue that you give up some useful experiences by not attending the same college for four or five straight years. I believe it is not where you start, but where you finish (as they say in sports).

Usually, classroom instruction itself does not make that big of a difference when it comes to getting a job and succeeding at it. What's important are all of the other experiences and skills you gain outside of the classroom. Simply put, a highly regarded, well-known college brand may help the job search by opening doors, but you can do other things, like networking and building contacts within your community, to maximize your chances of landing that first job within the corporate herd.

Myth: Grades Don't Really Matter.

Reality: Grades Do Matter, More So Early In Your Career.

As you've already learned, the college name may open doors, but grades are much more important in the early stages of your career. Poor grades will definitely keep you from getting a job, regardless of what college you graduated from. Let's face it, a G.P.A. speaks volumes about your work ethic; later in your career, 5-10 years down the road, experience is the dominant consideration by employers. Almost no one asks a corporate veteran about college grades, but then again, any honors from Summa to Magna look good in a curriculum vitae (or CV, a European term for a resume).

Myth: College is All I Need To Get Ahead.

Reality: Not Even Close.

You need to supplement your college "education" with other education to develop non-academic skills. The college curriculum is just a foundation that you need. The college degree is a "check off" item, meaning it is the minimum requirement to compete. You need to develop other skills. One of the most important skills is the ability to "connect the dots". It involves being creative, experienced, knowledgeable, and looking at things from other perspectives.

College degrees are academic knowledge, but not necessarily applied knowledge. Not all applied knowledge is learned through books or in the classroom. Applied knowledge requires creativity, experience, and implementation skills. As a manager, I noticed that early on in their careers, the employees in my organization with the most *applied* knowledge were more successful than the employees with all the *academic* achievements. Creativity is not taught in school or, for that matter, anywhere in the known practical world. Applied knowledge is basically showing what you can do. Academic knowledge is basically all that you know. As a manager, I'll take the person in the room that can get things done vs. choosing the smartest person in the room. I'm a big fan of implementation. Therefore, I believe that knowing how to do something is "where the rubber meets the road." You don't tell someone to turn on a creativity switch. As I observe these employees and read up on the topic, what I learned was that people who are creative are really doing two things most co-workers did not do:

1. looking at things from a different perspective
2. connecting ideas or approaches to form new ones

Creativity comes from getting inspiration. Inspiration comes from getting exposed to different situations, people, experiences, etc. It also comes from different venues, atmospheres, etc.

In short, you need to develop a desire and be open to gain a broader knowledge and broader experiences.

Here are some ways to broaden your overall education (academic AND applied):

- Be open to learn and experience broad topics. Be a young contrarian and learn things that people your age typically think is boring or useless or "old".

- Take continuing education courses.

- Gain a taste of corporate experience through internships, temporary jobs, summer jobs, and so forth.

- Get things done. Accomplish things. Complete projects and tasks.

- Learn to network …this is such an important topic I dedicated a chapter this subject (Chapter 13).

Myth: Internships Are a Waste of Time. It's Slave Labor.

Reality: Yes and no.

Internships have several great potential benefits: gain experience, sample industries/job function, network, secure a future job. I enthusiastically implore you to get one or more starting as soon as you can (high school), whether it's paid or non-paid, in whatever industry, and whatever job type that you desire. The key is to make the most of whatever internship you secure. There will be internships that are not very good. Companies may be disorganized or the job is not meaningful, or both. And in some cases, internships are free labor for the companies. Whatever the case, there is something to learn because that is exactly how the real corporate world environment is.

Related Story

A great example of applied knowledge or creativity was the story Steve Jobs, CEO of Apple Computer, told in a Stanford University commencement speech in 2005. Jobs used the term "connect the dots" as his advice to the graduates. Steve Jobs never graduated from college, yet he was a huge creative success. He told his audience that he took courses in college that interested him rather than those that were required for some degree. The courses he took had no apparent relationship…until years later at Apple. Jobs was touring Xerox's PARC facilities (Xerox Research & Development, where many of today's technologies were invented back in the 1970's and '80s) and was introduced to graphical user interfaces, high resolution screens, and the mouse controller. Xerox researchers were great technically, but awful at commercializing the technology. Jobs quickly saw an application (which would solve a weakness in the then current personal computer)–easier to use WYSIWYG ("what you see is what you get". Meaning what is displayed on the computer is what will print; all made possible through better graphics and typography.) The personal computer in the 1970's could not represent a printed page because the resolution was not there and font types could not be represented. Jobs understood this because he attended calligraphy classes in college (just for the fun of it). Thus the Macintosh was born and he targeted it to the graphics and advertising world. Together with Adobe, Apple launched the desktop publishing market that revolutionized many industries and lead to billions of dollars in profit.

As a manager, I learned that an employee who has a wide range of knowledge and experiences is more valuable. I would go to them if I needed a problem solver or needed to evolve the business (because they are more creative) compared to an employee that has been doing the same job/working at the same dept or company for a long time. The latter employee is fine for positions whose work does not need to change.

Unfortunately in today's corporate world, very few jobs are the latter; and almost no leadership positions are the same day in and day out.

The following is a list to help you put the recommendations in this chapter into practice.

Key Actions Checklist

- ☐ Get a college education. If you choose not to go to college, make sure you do something productive with your time.

- ☐ Whatever you do, do your best. For instance, if you're in college, get the best grades you can. If you have secured an internship opportunity, do your best to learn all that you can and perform well, even if you aren't being paid.

- ☐ Seek broad knowledge (and experiences), constantly, even topics that do not connect at the time. They will help enhance your resume now and later in your career it will help your creativity.

- ☐ Practice networking. Make extensive use of an electronic address book/contact management system. Focus efforts on the segment of people in your network who can be a mentor or can lead to career opportunities (such as internships, jobs, career advice, etc.).

- ☐ Get an internship to help you gain valuable experience.

Chapter 2 – Getting a Corporate Job (Getting into a Herd)

"Obstacles are there to see how badly you really want something"

~ Randy Pausch, Carnegie Mellon

Getting a job takes work and effort. There will be rejection and very little indication of progress along the way. In school, you are given a grade and teachers tell you how you're doing every step of the way. That's not the case with a job search. You have to be persistent. You have to be prepared. You have to practice a lot. Above all else though, you have to *want something more* than everyone else.

This may not be what you wanted to hear, but it's the truth and there's no point in sugar-coating it. As the opening quote above state so well, you have to put in the effort to get what you want.

But really, how do you get a job that requires experience when you need a job to get that experience?

Short answer:

- Develop your resume:
  - take inventory of your accomplishments (all accomplishments, not just work related). You should also assess your skills and really determine where you excel.
  - be creative in translating your accomplishments and skills into what corporate managers and the job calls for.
  - Don't do it all by yourself. Enlist help creating your resume and every step along the job-hunting process.
- Get the word out…advertise and sell, sell, sell.
- Get really good at interviewing.
- Go after internships.
- Get any work you can…it'll build experience, connections, and confidence.

Start with getting your resume together.

Your resume is your advertisement. It is the first of many times that hiring managers will learn about you. If you are young and lack true work experience, that just means that you need to work even harder to identify your skills and experiences that match what corporate managers are looking for and present them effectively in the resume.

Sidebar: There are lots and lots of books and information available on the topic of getting a job and interviewing. Read them, they're good. I'm not going to reinvent the wheel by writing yet another job hunting and interviewing book. I *am* going to cover what I consider to be the condensed version of the most poignant elements and mix in my perspective and experience. My slant on the job search and interviewing process is as both a person looking for a job and as a hiring manager. During my career at nine corporations, I landed three jobs during recessions - most recently during the worst recession in United States history (late 2010). Conversely, I've been a hiring manager for over 20 years, selecting a broad range of employee types: interns, entry-level positions, mid-level professional positions and management positions.

If you're like a lot of young people who were able to avoid real employment up until now, what do you do? Chances are you were spared real employment because your parents (like me and my wife) wanted our daughter to focus on her education and activities that kept her busy and allowed her to nurture her exceptional talent and interest. In our case, our daughter was a gifted music and theater performer. My wife and I had visions of our daughter on Broadway. Ask your parents. I'll bet they had visions of you doing something amazing. Perhaps they were hoping you'd turn out to be the next Jordan, Beckham, Picasso or Yoyo Ma. Most parents are content if their offspring excel at a professional career in Medicine, Engineering or Law.

For our daughter, and probably like a lot of young people, what she was good at was not what she eventually wanted to do for a living. So now we have a daughter with exceptional performing arts skills and no interest or innate skills in math, science, or business; a.k.a. the skills and desire necessary to make a predictable living. From a resume perspective, she spent most of her life accumulating experiences and skills that are not directly related to many corporate jobs.

How do young people like our daughter go about applying for a job when they have no direct employment experience? Here is what the previously unemployed should do:

- Highlight their performing arts skills as soft skills employers desire (look up the section in the book about hard and soft skills). For many employers, soft skills are more valuable because it is difficult, if not impossible, to teach soft skills to a human being.

- Highlight any social organizations he/she participated in and what accomplishments you have achieved. The key is to give examples of traits and skills that relate to or are success indicators for the position you are seeking. Examples include: project/task management, organization, self-initiative, decision-making, teamwork and collaboration, leadership, getting things done, positive energy, interpersonal communication, etc.

- Keep in mind that examples can include accomplishments at home.

- Work somewhere, anywhere, such as internships and volunteering, to develop and practice corporate hard skills and soft skills. Examples of hard skills include: specific subject-matter expertise like engineering, writing and intercommunications, project management, organization, computer applications. Soft skills include: being responsible, being reliable, having a positive attitude, etc.

- Get help creating/writing your resume. Have a skilled resume writer help you develop, or at least review, your resume. Take advantage of those "free" resume evaluations on the various job websites. Take advantage of your school's career center and those resume workshops and counselors. All these sources provide excellent, free services. The only time you may have to spend money is for someone to implement the suggestions and write your resume. If you don't have the writing skills or know someone who can do it for you, it is definitely worth the expense. You are short-changing yourself if you are writing your resume or having your parents do it for you if you know that it could be done better by a paid professional.

Getting the Word Out

It's time to get the word out and embark on your job search. Welcome to the World of Sales. Yes, you are a Sales rep now. If you thought Sales was some sleazy occupation and one that you vowed never to do, guess what? You're doing it! You are selling your employment services to potential customers or, in this case, you are selling yourself to corporations.

Myth: I *just need to sign up* for the Internet job websites.

Reality: You need to work harder than that. Unfortunately, it's just not that easy.

It is true that lots of jobs are posted on the Internet now. If you relied on that alone, however, you are competing with everyone else for the same positions. You are also just another unknown applicant. You need to get an edge. It could be a referral or a testimonial to jobs that have a limited number of applicants or jobs that are unlisted.

1. Network with people you know and enlist them to spread the word. Use every social and business network tool available (I.e. Facebook, Myspace, Linked-In, etc.). The whole concept and practice of Networking is so important. I mentioned networking early, I've mentioned it again here, and again I'll refer you to Chapter 13. As the sales and presentation cliché goes, "Tell them, tell them again, and then tell them what you told them". The key point I'll stress is – don't be embarrassed or ashamed to get your network to help out. You're dramatically increasing your chances and you're also learning *the* most important Sales skill (more on this in a later chapter). Get people to help you script out ways of asking that don't sound desperate or embarrassing. Short insight – you may think asking for help is all about you, but people may be helping themselves and their company by helping you. Many companies encourage their employees (possibly someone you know or your friends know in these companies) to bring in referrals, even to the extent of offering them a bounty if a referral is hired.

2. Apply directly on company websites. Some companies don't post their job openings on those popular job websites (because they have to pay a fee). Some companies will post it on their own websites and wait to post on outside job websites, perhaps to get applicants through their employees first. Company website postings are passive, meaning people have to find it and apply. Once it goes out to job websites, such as Monster.com, the job info is pushed out to people. So get an early jump on the job before it goes out to the world. Google search all the companies in your county. Go to their website and dig into the "Career" page. Some companies will have a page or path for entry level and internship applicants. For larger companies people recognize (such as Apple Computer), candidates send in thousands of

resume every month. Lesser known companies do not receive as many resumes. In either case, keep sending/posting your resume to the companies every 4 months. Some companies have acquired hardware and software to scan and input candidate resumes into their database so they can be searched against open positions, but the reality is that most companies do a horrible job with this or they don't use their database at all. One reason for this is that after 6 months, the resumes are deleted because they're simply not relevant.

3. Register with regional and national Temporary Agencies (such as Manpower, Volt, Kelly, etc.). The job does not have to be an internship, per say. Temp jobs are a great way to get your foot into a door. Find a Temp-to-Standard position through a placement agency (we also call it Temp-to-Perm, but in most States, companies are legally not using the term "permanent" to describe or classify a position. In their eyes, you are either a Temp, Contractor, or Standard employee). Most agencies have a permanent placement service and a temporary assignment service. The line is blurred. Fact is, you may have to start out as a temporary worker. It used to be that temporary placement agencies were used by companies for temporary help such as seasonal work, unforeseen demand load on a department, or for one-off projects. In the 1980's high tech firms used temporary agencies to supply "permanent" employees. High Tech firms were typically fast growing and their products had very short life cycles. These firms would receive a large influx of venture capital money and needed to staff up quickly. Temp-to-Perm became the norm in Northern California's High Tech industry. Soon other companies followed suite and used this approach because it offered the advantage of "testing out" a person. It's an easy way to handle bad hires. The Temp Agencies handled all the sourcing, screening, interviewing, background check, and payroll.

4. The reality is most people/companies are not good at hiring good people. It's time consuming. It takes an enormous amount of effort to coordinate and set up meetings. For every candidate interviewed, it takes hours of each interviewer's time to conduct the interviews, to write up assessments and then attend team meetings to discuss which candidate to hire. It's even more difficult and time-consuming to fire someone; more on this later. Bottom line is, if temps don't work out, just have the Temp Agency send more candidates; much easier and less legal risks

involved. As much as companies have created elaborate interviewing processes and spent millions on interviewing technique courses for their employees; most hiring managers are not very good at interviewing. It is much easier and revealing to see a candidate in action before making them an employee.

5. Use popular job websites such as Monster.com or Ladder.com. Companies use them to post for internships and part time help. Recruiters monitor job websites to gather applicant information to help them fill their client's current job openings, or for their own databases to use for future client job orders.

6. Check out the classified websites such as Craigslist. There are job listing here too. Craigslist is so inexpensive compared to the well-known job sites that many companies will only post jobs on this site. Companies like the fact that the respondents are local and most postings are for entry to mid-level jobs, part-time and full-time.

7. Join professional social networks like LinkedIn.com. Many companies will only post at these websites because they value the "relationship" and references candidates have with the LinkedIn network. Solicit recommendations from your LinkedIn contacts. Companies posting on LinkedIn are requiring applicants to have a minimum of two recommendations.

8. For you mid-career people: get involved with recruiters. Many companies use recruiters for specialized positions or difficult positions to fill, such as expertise knowledge or skill sets. Thus, many technical positions and leadership positions are sourced using recruiters. It's expensive to the company however. Recruiter's fees are between 20-30% of the job position's annual salary. One of the most valuable things that recruiters bring to the table is their ability to find and convince employed people to become a job candidate. A good recruiter has a database of people, their positions, and skill sets. Recruiters try to hire away candidates from their current employment or encourage them to provide people they know that might fit the position. With the Internet today, even junior recruiters build up their databases by searching job websites and by encouraging candidates to provide their resume. Therefore, you should network with recruiters. One way to do this is to identify recruiters/agencies from job listings, since many job openings are listed by recruiters for their client companies and not by the companies directly. Even if you are not a good fit, the recruiter will log you into their database for

other or future listings. Even after you are employed, it is a good idea to occasionally stay in touch with all the recruiters you gathered in your database. In fact, the best way to develop a relationship with recruiters is to provide them with possible candidates from your network. Several of my jobs came from recruiters and, in fact, one job came from a recruiter I had known for 5 years. There are Internet services that will mass blast your resume to all recruiters. I do not know how effective this is as there is little empirical data. You can do this yourself but it takes some time and effort. I believe the value is really a function of your skill set. Again, recruiters are used to locate specialized positions. If you are starting out early in your career, you probably do not fit most positions recruiters are working. But as mentioned, you are valuable to recruiters if you can refer people you know that are a good fit. In return, the recruiter will be valuable to you later.

Interview process

Hopefully at some point you receive a call about a position you applied for or, in some cases, for a position a recruiter finds for you. That's great! It's show time!

This is an extremely important phase. You probably think this is the easy part of the process. It can be for some people. However, I believe for most people, the interview phase is actually more difficult. Getting your resume together and getting the word out is very task-based. There's a certain recipe to follow and it does not involve people, and dealing with people is an art. People interaction is unpredictable. Effectively interacting and handling all possible variables involving people is not an exact science. The skills involved are soft and not those that people learn as they are growing up. It is situational; part art and part thinking on your feet, part adlibbing, part acting, part image and body language/ presentation. My best advice is: 1) get help and 2) practice, practice, practice.

Because there is so much already written about the interviewing process, I'll just touch on some key points to guide you through the process:

Get people to help you prepare and provide critique. Remember: even sports and entertainment superstars have coaches.

You need to be prepared. Prepare correctly so you are practicing the correct things. As previously mentioned (and worth mentioning again and again) – Practice, Practice, Practice and then practice some more. I cannot emphasize this enough.

Read through some of those interview books and Google "how to answer interview questions" columns on the Internet. Search for "top ten interview questions" and get your answers down pat. You should have the "elevator speech" ready anytime you are asked those FAQ (frequently asked questions) about you and your qualifications. In other words, if you were to ride an elevator with a recruiter for 10 floors, you should be able to tell the recruiter why you are a good hire in about 3 sentences. What's the #1 question asked in interviews? – it's " *What can you tell me about yourself?*" Since you only have 3 sentences, you're not going to give a life story starting with your days in high school! Your reply should be natural and confident (which is why you should practice, practice, practice). With every reply, you should illustrate a skill and accomplishment. You will know you are successful with your reply if the interviewer/stranger asks a follow-up question to get more details about your accomplishments.

Read the books and articles on how to interview someone (not just how *to be* interviewed). You may be surprised to learn what interviewers are taught (and how much they don't use). In summary, interviewers are taught to probe using the technique of taking a topic, such as something on your resume, and then asking rounds of questions about the topic. Each round of questions digs deeper into the topic to uncover your involvement, contribution, and accomplishments. For example, if your resume has indicated you were President of your Sorority, the interviewer will start with a general probing questions such as "What were your duties as President?" You might reply that you lead development of the agenda and budget for the year. The interviewer will then ask, "How did you go about the development?" As you provide answers, the interviewer will ask more specific, deeper probing questions about the answer and request details such as names, dates, approach, results, tools used, etc. Knowing the tricks of a good interviewer will help you. If you find yourself with an interviewer who is practicing good interviewing techniques, you will be better prepared with replies that are factual and accomplishment-based. Getting inside the head of the interviewer and turning the tables on yourself when preparing for an upcoming interview will give you a valuable edge.

Always be auditioning. Remember, ALL phone calls from a recruiter or human resource specialists are basically interviews! You are being interviewed when you park your car in the company's parking lot, when you walk into the lobby, when you are waiting for your interviewer, when you are offered lunch and so on. What you say and how you say it (verbal and body language-wise) is an interview reply. Therefore, do what they do in show business: prepare for auditions. Practice with someone; practice in front of a mirror; practice with a video camera. It's embarrassing at first, but you would rather know now and make the adjustments in your living room, than at the interview. And no matter how good you think you are, there is always something to learn by seeing yourself on a video screen.

Myth: Never discuss salary in the 1st interview.

Reality: It is perfectly fine to discuss this topic.

Despite some misconceptions about when to bring up salary in an interview process, I believe it is perfectly fine for hiring managers and HR people to bring up salary requirements on the first interview. It doesn't have to be an exact figure. Either party can and should share the range they require. Hiring team members don't want to waste the organization's time if the candidate's demands are completely out of the budget range of the position. Rarely do companies, especially the medium to large ones, make exceptions outside of the budget set for the position. It is the job of Human Resources to properly research the salary comparisons for the position. A company will only change if they realize, after several interviews, and with other supporting information, that the position's compensation was incorrectly set. And if that was the case, it takes some work on the department manager's behalf to find additional money in the budget. Understand that most hiring managers do not have carte blanche to sign off on an offer. He/She must get approval from a Finance Analyst/Mgr, an HR Rep/Mgr, and his Manager/VP. If you, the candidate, are asked what salary requirement you have, you should provide a realistic one or simply turn the question around and ask what range the position is budgeted for. Don't hem or haw about it or try to be coy. This is the first interview. It is not a negotiation. If you are the best candidate and the company wants to hire you, you will have something to negotiate and there will be time. Playing a game this early in the process is a deal-killer.

Call Back!...They've Asked You Back For More Interviews

As you progress through the interview process and you reach the second or third round of interviews, the situation begins to look promising. Organizations at this point are trying to decide between two or three final candidates. Organizations may involve additional interviewers, generally people from other departments the position will interact with or peers of the hiring manager.

At this point in the interview process, the organization is looking for one of the following to help them decide on the candidate they ultimately want to make an offer to:

- **Which candidate is the best "fit" with business skills and personality?** The interviewer, (this person is probably from a department that will work with the candidate's department and likely the candidate directly) is looking to see if they are *comfortable* with the candidate. You need to help the interviewer feel comfortable with both your business ability AND your personality style. To provide a response to the business skills and business interaction you need to understand what your interviewer's role is, so ask the person at the beginning of the interview. It is appropriate to ask for the titles of each interviewer in advance. If you don't receive it, you will have to tailor and respond "on-the-spot." In short, you need to help the interviewer believe: a) you will be easy to work with; b) you will be responsive; c) you will support the workflow (whether it is a formal one or an informal one); and d) you will help her/him achieve their goals. With respect to personality style, you need to be cordial, friendly, and find a common interest with the interviewer. A helpful approach is to match personality styles with your interviewer. There are many books and seminars about this concept, the two more popular being the *Myers-Briggs* and *DISC* personality assessment. I encourage you to do the research.

- **Questionable areas requiring more probing.** The interview team had questions or uncovered areas they were uncomfortable with or required clarity. Follow-up interviews often are used to probe deeper or to get clarification. Typically members of the initial interview team, such as the hiring manager or the HR representative, will be the interviewer. New interviewers may be used and they would be coached to probe the questionable areas. For example, we interviewed many candidates that were living outside of California. We were always concerned that the high cost of living would be an issue. With most positions, it was unrealistic to raise the base salary or provide bonuses and/or relocation to make up the difference. As a result, the candidate (and his/her family) might experience a reduced quality of life if they accepted the offer. To prevent wasting everyone's time, we would probe this topic from many angles to make sure the candidate(s) would accept the offer if made to him/her. You would be surprised how difficult it was to get an honest answer and there was never enough time to get it in the early interview rounds. So, these follow up interviews were a good way to ensure that we were making the right choice when it came to our prospective candidate.

Turn The Table…Time For You to Ask The Questions!

The real fun begins when you notice that the interviewers have run out of questions and are expecting you to ask them questions. Or better yet, they begin to sell you on why the company/job is desirable. I recommend at this point that you interview them. Up to this stage of the process, the ball has been in the company's court to find a candidate that fits. They may tell you about the company and about the job, but their goal is to find the candidate they want to make an offer to. It's your turn now. As excited as you might be, use this time to interview them. This will reinforce or solidify their judgment of your candidacy and your eagerness to work for them. This is also a great time to get a early jump on your job success. Turn the table and probe to learn about your manager and all the people you will be working with, what their personalities styles are, what they expect, how they behave, and so forth.

Tony's Stories

When I was interviewing for one of my past positions, I asked the hiring manager for a list of people who reported to him so I could chat with them and learn more about his management style. Yes, I asked him for references! He was initially shocked but he gave me several contacts. He was also impressed, which lead to me getting an offer. I also gained incredible insight into what I could expect with my new manager and some keys to be successful with him. After joining the company, I heard numerous times, from many in the organization, how they couldn't figure out my manager, but they noticed I had him figured out and that I worked so well with him. They all did not know the special bond I created and the insight I received very early on that accelerated my ability to be successful.

Don't Despair. Don't Give Up

The most difficult part about job hunting is the waiting and helplessness. You have to keep plugging away. It's not easy to keep motivated, but you have to find ways. Keep up a routine of checking job sites, following up with friends and family, and keep working all avenues. As with any sales campaign, it is a numbers game. As a sales rep, I was taught it takes 100 cold calls to get 10 appointments and from those appointments, one sale. The point is you have to keep working the numbers to give yourself a chance. While you're waiting to hear back from an interviewer continue to search for jobs, and never assume that you got the position, as this will put you behind in the job hunting process should you find out that they passed on you later on.

In the meantime, you have to keep yourself prepared for interviews because you don't want to blow an opportunity, especially if they are far and few between. Get people to review your resume and cover letters. Keep practicing your interview answers. Review interviews from jobs you did not get offers for with someone to get feedback to improve for next time. In fact, ask the recruiter and interviewers what areas they felt the winning candidate had over "those" not hired.

I was lucky enough to rarely experience tough times. Several of my jobs came from friends referring me and assisting in the background. On one occasion, the economy was so red hot that I had five job offers within 30 days. And one position that I secured through a recruiter, who I stayed in touch with over a 3-year period, was for a job two miles from my current work just at the time I really needed to make a change.

Myth: There are general time frames to land a job for each job level.

Reality: All the general rules are out the window.

For the foreseeable future, the job market has never been more competitive and unpredictable. The recession and global economy has created new obstacles and enlarged traditional obstacles for job seekers. That being said, you have to be more prepared and do *everything* better – increase your skill set, illustrate your accomplishments and soft skills, be more flexible about job location, engage others to help you and, last but not least, set your expectation. As the saying for this chapter states – expect obstacles, but go after them because you want to succeed more than everyone else. There will be failures. There will be rejections. The process can be long. The thing to remember is: don't get discouraged. Instead, figure out what you need to improve and keep working the process.

Tony's Stories

The first story took place in 2001 after 9/11 and the world, along with the economy, was reeling. I was going through layoffs at Gateway, but I was not overly concerned, because in the past I've always been able to generate job opportunities very quickly due to my strong resume and background. After all, my background included many well-known corporations and my experience had progressed steadily. I received an early interview with a company I was very interested in and had an initial phone interview. To my surprise and disappointment, I never received a follow up interview. This happened again with another interested company. I realized the following: **1) I was not in interview-shape and 2) I was too arrogant about my background.** I had been out of the job market for some time. I had not practiced my interviewing skills. I did not have the answers to the top ten interview questions down pat. I thought that being a Director and having a resume with great company pedigree was enough for companies and recruiters to hand me job offers. Wow, what a rude awakening for me!

The second story took place recently, December 2010, in the middle of the worst recession since 1930. In Orange County, California the unemployment rate was over 10%. The number of Director level or higher positions were scarce, but I was able to land a Director position with little effort in a few months. I went job-hunting because I wanted to make sure the insights I'm sharing were still relevant. I followed everything in this book – from updating the format of my resume; using an outside reviewer; using all of my social network; using job websites; engaging recruiters and, finally, to the key element I keep stressing – **I practiced my interviewing skills.** It all paid off.

You Got An Offer!

Generally you will get strong indications that an offer is being prepared for you. If you're working with a good recruiter, they already know and will clue you in. If not, you will get obvious and sometimes not so obvious hints. Being asked for references alone is not obvious. Depending on the company, they may ask all top candidates for references because the candidate given the first offer may turn down the job. I know it is hard to believe in tough economic times, but it can happen. And during good economic times, when skilled candidates are scarce, I saw rejection rates of 40%.

As previously mentioned, many hiring managers are simply terrible at the interview process and they will just flat out tell you that they would like to have you on board and are working on an offer. The managers that are "good" at this process will never make a commitment because there is always the chance of legal action if they make a "verbal offer." Instead, they will make "trial closes" to make sure they have an offer that will secure your acceptance (and avoid the haggling game). "Trial close" is a term used in sales to see if a "customer" will "buy the product and to uncover your objections." In this case they will ask about salary, benefits, start date, and any other requirements needed for you to accept the position and to start soon.

This is where you can use the trial close technique as well. A word of caution, unlike in the movies, most job positions are not the type where all sorts of demands can be made. As expected, the higher the position the more items can be requested and negotiated. I suspect most of you reading this are just starting out or in a mid-level position. Therefore, the positions will have little room for demands and negotiations. With that being said, for things you can request, you should not be afraid to ask. It's *how* you ask, not just *what* you ask for, thus the use of the "trial close" technique is important. Trial close is more about asking questions rather than making demands. Here's an example of a trial close regarding salary, *"I appreciate the $35,000 a year offer. It is fair and in the range. Is there flexibility in the budget to increase the salary offer to $38,000?"* The trial close is not a demanding approach that puts the hiring manager in an ultimatum position. I have seen many brash candidates demand requirements and/or make demands that are so out of bounds that the hiring manager cannot get approval for them.

When you receive the offer letter, hopefully you'll find that it is anti-climatic because you've worked the process correctly. Nevertheless, opening an offer letter is surreal in a pleasant way because at one point you were trying so hard to convince a company that you are a valuable asset to them. Then somewhere along the way, the table turns and now they are desperate to convince you to join them.

You Accept The Offer!

- Let out a scream of joy.

- Send a handwritten "thank you" to anyone that helped you, such as the recruiter, any mentors who helped you practice your interview answers, the temp agency representative you got the job lead from, and so on. Emails are acceptable too, according to a recent CareerBuilder survey (Orange County Register article, April 27,

2011), but there is something very personal and unique about a handwritten note in this day and age.

- Ask your new company about your Human Resource contact and your new supervisor what you can do prior to your starting date. Is there a business plan to read? Are there marketing materials, presentations, research reports to read before starting that will bring you up to speed on what the company is doing? Are there events or trade shows to attend that will help introduce you to some of your new coworkers and the industry?

Key Actions Checklist

☐ Read up on articles and books about job searches, interviewing, and successful job hunting.

☐ Create/Develop/Refine your resume. Get your resume evaluated.

☐ Get the job search going. Tap into all of the various avenues mentioned.

☐ Do your homework prior to an interview. Learn everything about the company. Make a list of questions you can ask the interviewer(s). Develop and practice your answers to the top 10 interview questions.

☐ Practice. Practice. And keep practicing. Can you answer the most popular opening interview question, "Tell me about yourself", smoothly, confidentially, and sincerely?

Chapter 3 – Got the job
(First Days In The Herd)

"You have one chance to make a first impression." ~ Unknown

You're hired! You're a member of a herd now. Congrats.

These first few weeks are a great time because you have no deadlines or demands by others. Basically no one knows you exist yet. *You're in a training period.* The company is excited to have you on-board because you're needed. You feel great because the feeling of being wanted is intoxicating. Getting your ego stroked is quite a high, so enjoy it. This is why everyone calls it the honeymoon period. The relationship is positive both ways and both parties have nothing to complain about – no stress, no criticism, no pressure, no demands, just all high expectations.

Don't Let Your Guard Down

For the first few weeks, before anyone knows about you, before people know your phone number/extension, your email, and before your boss has assigned anything to you, you're going to have lots of time and little responsibility. *Just because these times may appear carefree doesn't mean that you should let your guard down.*

Chances are:

- there will be no formal training;
- no one will take you under their wings;
- there will be no formal orientation or agenda

Use this time to make a good impression with everyone you meet and with your boss.

The Do's and Don'ts to make the first impression a positive (and lasting) one.

Dos':

- **Heed this famous sales axiom:** "You only get one chance to make a first impression." The statement is obvious to some degree, but is so well stated. On the surface, you need to be presentable. It is still better to be overdressed than under dressed at the workplace. Men: always wear a collared shirt and slacks. Carry a tie (men) and a second outfit (women) and leave it in your car or cubicle just in case. It is better to be conservative and professionally smart. Worst-case scenario, if you did not know the dress culture at your new company, you will after the first few introductions. You can always race back to dress down or dress up if needed. It may not need to be said, but make sure you have good hygiene. Store a toothbrush and toothpaste in your car or drawer, and be sure to carry some breath freshener with you at all times (mints or gum are great).

- **Greet people by their name.** When you are first introduced to someone new, learn their name and its correct pronunciation. One trick is to repeat it back to that person and ask if you said it correctly. Repeating their name will help you remember it. Another old trick is to find something about the person that links their name such as a rhyme or description. For example, you just met a Larry and he has little hair on his head. So Larry is "not hairy." It is perfectly fine to ask for their business card (yes, even if they are fellow employees) and write on the back of the card how you met them and at least 1-2 points of interest. Try different techniques to help you remember people's names.

- **Practice good manners and be respectful.** When someone extends their hand to shake, you should make a firm (not crushing), confident, genuine handshake at first introduction. Smile. Be respectful of every person regardless of their rank or role. I cannot tell you how many times I saw this old saying actually happen, "your peers could be your boss one day." Short term, you will be surprised how helpful people are even though their rank or role may seem "low and useless." More on this later. Reply to questions that will be mostly small talk. On that note, be genuine, confident, and respectful in everything you do at this point, period. No exceptions.

- **Consult Executive Administrators.** You will have lots of questions and many you will think are too petty to ask your boss or all the hard working people around you. So don't take that risk by asking them. Ask the executive administration instead (or in the old days, they called this position "secretaries"). They know everything and everyone. Their title may fool you. They are more than simple administrators. They are really the Junior Vice President/Office Manager/Human Resource/Facilities gurus all rolled into one.

Don'ts:

- **Don't try to be the life of the party.** Think of yourself as the guest at a party, not the host. You're just a new employee, not a celebrity.

- **Don't talk too much and listen too little.** Another business saying states it perfectly, "you have two ears and one mouth." At the initial introduction, whether one-on-one or in a group setting (and that includes initial staff meetings), you will build a better image if you are less talkative, listen and observe more. You are in learning mode. There is also a great benefit from getting others to talk to you and tell you about themselves and what they do – they feel better about you because you made them feel better about themselves. People love to talk about themselves. You'll gain a fan because you expressed an interest in what they do and you allowed them to brag a bit. Listening more and talking less is really hard for some people to do. Some of you are naturally shy or non-talkative so you will default to this at this stage of your career in the company. This accidental behavior is a safety default.

  Some of you, however, are on the other end of the continuum. You cannot help yourself. I cannot stress how hard you must resist the temptation to talk. I have the disease and battled it all my life. When I was in kindergarten, my mom said I was put in the corner a lot because I talked too much. Here are typical examples of what I've heard from new employees I've met – excessive small talk, jump into business talk, brag about where they went to school, brag about where they worked before, share improvement opportunities they see in the company already, how they use to do something at their last employment, etc. As the new employee, you will have time and better ways to share all that. I'm not saying you shouldn't build relationships at work. But this is too much, too soon.

- **Don't over estimate how important you *really* are.** Enduring the interviewing period and ending up with an offer is extremely exhilarating and a real ego booster. It's great to feel wanted. You imagine going to work on the first day and expect banners and signs and a welcoming committee. WAKE UP! Once you start the job, the courting is over. Don't be disillusioned. That's just how things work. Keep your expectations low. Don't expect everyone you meet to look at you as the savior. Even if you are going to relieve their workload, most people are busy with their own responsibilities and you may be a distraction away from whatever they are doing.

As the new person, you may even be a burden initially as they have to train you and tolerate your learning curve.

The 100 Day Plan

It is odd, but most organizations have an "assimilation program" for senior managers, but not for lower level jobs. Using a football analogy, the assimilation plan helps an employee get familiar with the team and the game: it's players, player's numbers, player's positions/functions, organization's policy and culture, and its support structure. Don't wait for someone to handhold you through the initial assimilation or orientation process. Take the initiative and create a plan.

Outline a plan of what you want to accomplish in the first 100 days on the job – we'll call it the 100 Days Plan. Start with the goals of the position you gathered from your hiring manager and others on the hiring team. Your direct manager should have a set of goals written or at the very least verbally communicated in a clear manner. And if you paid attention, and asked probing questions during the interviews, you would have gained valuable insight that can help to elaborate upon the goals, define new ones, or identify tasks associated with the goals.

For the first few weeks, your plan would obviously involve mostly general housekeeping items such as:

1. getting introduced to fellow employees, especially key co-workers, team members, key departments

2. getting familiar with the facilities (finding out where the various departments within the building are located and such)

3. getting your workspace set up

4. basic company policies and processes, such as getting a computer, an email account, forms for expenses and time cards (companies still use this in this 21st century) and so forth, proper parking area, etc. With some companies, you may be handed a Company Policy manual/binder

5. schedule for training if necessary (depends on the type of job)

The remaining weeks of the plan should involve the actual workings of your position and what action plan and tasks are needed to accomplish your goals. This will involve the following:

- Reviewing documents and files relevant to your projects and goals.

- Attending detailed meetings with key individuals that will play a role in your ability to accomplish your goals.

- Identify specific tactics for accomplishing the goals and the details that define your job function and its goals.

Key Actions Checklist

☐ Do all you can to make a good first impression. Make sure you're well dressed and well groomed.

☐ Make notes on every person you meet. Say their name somewhere in your greeting and/or departure.

☐ Respect everyone.

☐ Listen more. Talk less.

☐ Develop a 100 Days Plan.

Chapter 4 – Brand You
(No cow pun intended)

"Image is Everything" ~ Canon commercial slogan.

You may be wondering why we're spending so much time this early in your job (and career) discussing image and trying to develop a positive, influential, and productive one? It is because, as an old camera commercial slogan states, "Image is EVERYTHING."

In 1999, Tom Peters, a well published management guru, released *the* must-read book *The Brand You*. Just as name-brand products convey a certain deliverable that consumers expect and trust, you are in a perfect position to create a deliverable about you to the new organization (and external organizations you may interact with).

Your brand is, essentially, what defines you in the corporate world. It is what you want to portray to others and describes you and what you can accomplish in the workplace and beyond. The brand is the "promise" of what people can expect and trust from the product or service. The product is YOU and what YOU deliver. A person's brand can convey integrity. Are you punctual, accurate, reliable, creative, a problem-solver, a team player, etc.? Your brand will make you stand out from the herd; just like on a supermarket shelve, people recognize the brand names and have preconceived EXPECTATIONS of quality and price. Your brand will raise you above the herd and all the day-to-day "noise" at work.

Bottom-line. The people in a position to promote others do not have the time to notice all that happens within the crowded herd. Managers and Executives have minutes to devote to any subject. You want to be on their *short list*. You want to be a name they know among the hundreds and thousands among the herd. When people want a soda, they don't say soda. They ask for a Coke. A brand can be positive or negative or can stand for certain attributes. Apple products are viewed as hip, cool, easier to use and expensive. Windows-based personal computers are viewed as buggy, but much less expensive.

A positive brand image takes time to develop but a very short time to destroy. Look what happened with Toyota. And turning a negative image around is VERY difficult, if not improbable. You develop your brand with a combination of things you do AND things you DO NOT do. We discussed some of the DON'T Dos. Here are some things you do that help to define your brand:

Be Consistent

Business people hate people and events that are unpredictable. Conversely, co-workers and your superiors will respect and positively view those employees who are consistent in how they work, because business people and leaders want to plan things out and see that the plans are executed as planned. Therefore, if you are consistent in what you say, do, AND act out, they can plan around you and know the outcome that will likely occur.

Pay Attention to Detail

Earlier in this decade, there was a best selling book called *Don't Sweat the Small Stuff*. Then a best selling book, *Sweat the Small Stuff*, contradicted the earlier book. They're both correct…you have to do both, but you also have to know when to apply them at just the right moment. When you are in a strategy meeting or brainstorming session, don't fixate on the details. However you cannot ignore the small stuff when it's time to implement a task or when handling your daily interaction, such as communications. "Small stuff" means not simply dealing with the small stuff, but also ensuring that you are doing it right. If you're going to do the work, do it well. That applies to the small stuff. For example, you have an email from a co-worker. The subject of the email is low in your priority. If you ignore the email and don't respond, your "brand" will be known as a person who does not respond to emails. So you reply half-heartedly, and hastily, with a response that is not productive. You do not address the person's request completely or you do not meet up to expectations, and you leave the door open to more trivial emails from this person.

Be Organized and Stay On Top of Follow-Ups

Perception is reality. If your desk is a mess, people will think, and thus believe, that you are disorganized. They will look for and/or remember the one time you forgot something and that will, therefore, be the legacy of your brand…the person who is disorganized. Keeping your workspace tidy may seem like small stuff, but I would argue that this is small stuff worth doing. One of the challenges I had in the corporate world, even as a Director, was how I had to keep on top of people and tasks I delegated. You would think the mere fact that a superior ranked person personally delegated tasks and a due date to a subordinate would be enough to insure the completion of the task.   NOT. If you are the subordinate, you want to create a brand that states you are reliable and your supervisors will not have to keep chasing you around for status reports or updates or even timely deliveries. Most of your co-workers will not have this brand. When you become a supervisor, or if you are a subordinate but are relying on someone else's work in order to complete your task, stay on top of those people. Get a system or tool in place to help you. I used my electronic calendar on both my Smartphone and my laptop and listed the delegated items as to-dos with dates to remind me to follow up. I would schedule intermittent meetings, in advance, for status reports or operations reviews.

Be Positive, But Not Unrealistic

Being positive does not mean that you have to be a cheerleader or to wear rose-colored glasses. It also does not mean ignoring damaging situations. Being positive, at a minimum, means NOT being negative. Refrain from negativity and sarcasm. Live your life with a good attitude. This applies to your corporate life too. This philosophy should be very obvious, so I'm not going to dwell on it much. There are scores of books and articles about the power of a positive attitude. I will say this: if you maintain a good attitude, look for opportunities and ideas, and get things done effectively, you have a better chance of getting ahead in the corporate world.

Negativism and cynicism seem to rear their ugly heads as people get "older" at a job or company. I used to have a five-year warning for myself. By the fifth year in a job or company, it is very natural to become complacent, critical, and cynical. The newness of the job or company has long since worn off. You've had a chance to see the typical ugliness of any organization, because, as we mentioned earlier, people can and will do bad things. You may see departments or employees not doing their jobs; executives cutting costs, but giving themselves fat bonuses; HR enacting annoying policies, and so on. Some long-term employees like to have "bitch" sessions at lunch. I was very conscious of the possibility of getting drawn into the negativity, and worked to avoid it. You should too. If you are effective at avoiding the negativity, your "brand" will be positive, and you will stand out to your management.

Be The Repair Person, Not The News Reporter or Consultant

Be fixated on implementing solutions, not in identifying problems. It's easy to be a reporter. Everyone is a critic. It doesn't take much effort. Funny thing is most employees think and feel really smart when they are uncovering problems. And they think everyone will think they are smart for always reporting to everyone about what's wrong. *As you'll soon see, creating an effective solution to a problem is more creative and appreciated than merely discovering a problem.*

Reporters don't really add value to an effective corporate culture. In fact, reporters are a dime a gazillion. They are everywhere. They are a commodity. There are reporters among your co-workers, your company's vendors, your company's investors, and your company's customers. A small handful will attempt to offer solutions. These are the consultants. The problem is that many consultants are news reporters trying not to look like critics. So they try (or pretend) to be a consultant, but their solutions are worthless because they are not well thought out and cannot be implemented effectively. An old saying sums up this concept: "Ideas are plenty. Implementation is key." It's not hard to come up with ideas. The hard work is creating a solution for a problem, and executing the idea correctly. In short, to enhance your brand with management, *be the person who has ideas and knows how to implement them.*

Be A Sponge

Don't stop learning. Just because it is not your job, doesn't mean your should not learn the process anyway. Just because you don't like something, it doesn't mean that you should not learn to appreciate it. You don't have to become an expert. Familiarity with a broad range of topics and knowledge will help you in many ways. The better you understand how various business functions work, i.e. how they interact and challenges they face, the better problem solver and team player you will be. Having a more comprehensive perspective will make you appear bright, smart, empathetic and collaborative. And those are some key qualities for a standout to have in the corporate world.

Don't Assume

There's a popular axiom in business: "Don't Assume…it makes an ASS of U and ME." One way to demonstrate an innovative nature is to never assume anything. Question (literally and figuratively) existing processes and the reason they exist and operate as they do. Try to understand all points of view. Don't question in a demeaning, condescending, or cynical way. You want to ask in an inquisitive way, requesting consultation from your fellow employees. People love to be consulted. And when you ask the right questions, you avoid assuming, thereby avoiding inaccuracies, mistakes, and wasted time.

Be Reliable

Reliability means delivering what people need and expect on time. To put it simply: "say what you will do and do what you say." It means being at meetings on time and providing deliverables when you promised them. (And if you cannot deliver on-time, keep people in the loop with a status report well in advance of the meeting or due date.)

Be a Great Communicator

I use to joke that English was a second language for me. People would laugh, but the truth is I used it as an excuse to allow myself to mispronounce words or use poor grammar instead of putting in the effort to improve my communications skills. After all, my parents immigrated to the United States when I was 5 years old so I had ample time to master the English language. The wake-up call for me was when I had to take "bone head" English in my first year of college because I did not pass the English proficiency test.

I spent my entire professional career working on many communication flaws. You don't stop working at it. How you communicate is such a defining part of your Brand and success that I've devoted the next chapter to it.

Key Actions Checklist

☐ Review the book, *The Brand You,* by Tom Peters.

☐ Write down the Brand characteristics you want to be known for in the work place. Live them, improve them, and refine them all the time.

☐ Read this chapter again right after you start your new job.

Chapter 5 – Commooonication Skills

"Talk is cheap" ~ Unknown

Communication skills are very important because people judge you by *what* you communicate and *how* you communicate – speaking, writing, and body language. And there are so many more ways to communicate: face-to-face and remotely using Skype, over the phone, email, text, and even a good old fashioned letter delivered via postal or fax. Yes, "talk" is cheap and easy to do. Surprisingly, communication is actually difficult to do well.

I'm not as focused on the content of what you communicate; this book is focused more on the "how." I would submit that you *can* convey a good image of yourself if you are a great communicator even if your content is marginally good. The opposite does not hold true and would be embarrassing, and even disastrous, to your image. In several places throughout this book, we've already talked about presentation skills and refining those skills. Those are the foundations or basics to success: Practice, practice, practice.

Business communication is Formal

Stay professional. Get to the point – issue, action, results, etc. And don't write like you're texting someone. Limit or avoid using emoticon (e.g. Smiley faces ;-). Write complete sentences. Use graphics and pictures in a professional way to support your communications. For example, a graph is great to show your sales performance for the last three months. But you can skip the cute picture of your dog. Use proper English and grammar. Everything you do is a reflection and projection of your brand/image.

Communications and Emotion

Always buy yourself time to let emotions cool and allow your non-emotional or logical side to take over before you speak or write anything to someone. This rule is especially true in a professional setting.

You cannot take back what you say. Enough said on that. Written words do not convey emotion like spoken words. So a golden rule is: *Never use email or text to communicate anything emotional and sensitive.* Emails and text are quick and easy to use, but they must be used with care and caution.

Words and phrases, and how you convey them, can be very powerful for negative and positive effect. When you leave or send a handwritten note to someone to say, "good job", the impact is positive and lasting. On the contrary, two phrases to avoid are "why…?" and "do you have to…" Both are very direct and accusatory. If you need someone to explain themselves, such as in the case of a poor decision or action, instead of "why did you do that?" or "do you have to do that…?", use "how come…?" or " what lead you to that?" or ""how would you have done that differently…?".

Typically conveying emotions with words is best left to an accomplished fictional writer. Alas, we all must write or respond to an emotional situation or topic in the corporate world. That being the case, wait a day before writing or saying anything. Write your response or what's on your mind but don't send it for another day. Hours or days later, reread what you wrote and, if you believe the message will be productive, hit the "send" button. Writing out (or scripting) what you want to say is also a good practice when you want to communicate verbally to someone about an emotional subject or situation.

If you must write to someone about an emotional topic, do your best to think about how people reading your written communications might interpret the emotion behind your words. You can use a variety of styling and symbols to make your message as clear as possible. For example, use CAPS to "shout" out something. Use the color red to emphasize a point. And so forth. The technology allows for all this, so use it.

Avoid a Trail – Don't Write Emails/Memos or Leave a Voicemail

If you have anything emotional, sensitive, or controversial to discuss with someone, do it in person. For one, these situations always require interaction, so it's easier to do in person immediately rather than several email or voicemails that may brew over time and make the situation even worse. As stated above, chances are you will never correctly articulate in writing what you are trying to get across. Lastly, you don't want the communication passed around and misinterpreted by someone other than the person you intended.

Don't Hit the Send Button so Quickly

Read all communications at least twice. You'll be surprised how often you'll find grammar and spelling errors (even if your system has spellchecker; it doesn't catch everything). Make sure the message reads back like you intended. And make sure you look at the send-to address fields. The common mistake is to hit "reply all." This makes you look careless to all the unintended recipients. More importantly, make sure "politically" that the right people are receiving the message. Make use of the CC: and BCC: fields when you want to make sure other people are in the know because you want to cover yourself.

Thee Email Rule

I had a rule with my staff…if your emails with someone exceeds three replies cycles, stop the emails and get together in person (in other words, an email is started between two people and one person reply's to the other person's reply who replied to the original email). Get together, have an exchange of conversation, get clarity, and collaborate to solve any problems that may have arisen. My reasoning for this was:

1. There's probably going to be a mis-understanding, confusion or wrong information exchanged.

2. Too much time will be spent in all the iterations.

3. Too much latent time will transpire (time between replies will increase).

Throwing People Under The Bus

This is a common term in the corporate world to describe blaming (rightly or wrongly) someone for a mistake. The advice here is to be very careful and avoid throwing someone under the bus verbally or in written form. It is common in the corporate world to point fingers at perceived failures. As the saying goes, "if you have nothing nice to say, don't say anything at all".

Don't Multi-Task While Communicating

It's tempting…writing, reading, or talking on the phone while doing other things or doing all of the above at the same time. Being able to multi-task is a way to save time. Maybe, but are you really doing everything well? You think you are being efficient with your time, but you are actually wasting time. I guarantee you will write poorly. You will mis-read a message. And you will not comprehend what someone is saying over the phone, and the person on the other end will easily realize they don't have your full attention. You will end up spending time correcting mistakes, doing damage control because of mis-communications, and repeating conversations. Ultimately, preventing damage to your image is more important than your perceived gains in time.

Key Actions Checklist

☐ Be professional, especially with your communications. Leave the informal practice out of the office. Don't communicate like you're still in college or with friends. Don't write like you're texting someone.

☐ Always re-read any written communications (including email) before sending. Emails should be professional too. Make sure it's well written; be concise yet provide enough detail to be useful. Use the proper tone and format the communication so it is easy for the reader to read.

☐ Practice good email protocol. Include the right people (or leave out irrelevant ones). Sometimes, face-to-face is better than an email.

☐ Take communications seriously. Stay focused. Avoid multi-tasking while doing communications (i.e. emails, writing memos, talking on the phone).

Chapter 6 – Bottom Grazers, Move Ahead

"There are no menial jobs, just menial attitudes." ~ William John Bennett

Let's get back to breaking ahead of the herd. You've begun a new job and, for many of you, this is the first job in your "career." Many of these first jobs are really low-level, "entry positions", as the corporate world likes to call them. You may be working in a call center among hundreds of other co-workers doing exactly what you are doing. Or you might be an Accounting Clerk in an Accounting department with 20 other Accounting Clerks. I get the point. I used to manage call centers with nearly 100 customer service agents making less than $12/hour. You believe your job doesn't allow you the time or latitude to differentiate yourself. You're probably reading this book at this point and thinking to yourself: self, "I don't think a lot of these tips apply to me because my job is so low on the food chain.".

But you are so wrong young herd member; most of these tips do apply to you. Your level of incompetence and lack of useful corporate knowledge is all that's keeping you from getting ahead. It's up to you. Therefore, keep gaining knowledge, skills, insights, tips, etc. Separating yourself from the herd is even more important at low-level jobs because there are so many more people at that level.

First Things First – Do Your Job Well

It doesn't matter that your job is beneath you. I'm sure you can do your job in your sleep. Yes, a vast majority of entry-level jobs are not ultra challenging. Get past all that. Getting ahead of the herd starts with what you do, not just what your potential is. Do your job better than everyone else. Everything else builds upon this. It was amazing to me just how shortsighted most people in these positions are, especially young people. Don't look at your current job as the end-all. It's a stepping-stone. It can lead to other opportunities. We'll discuss job and career path in more detail later. In the meantime, the bottom line is this – you drastically limit any opportunities if you are a poor performer. Superiors identify and monitor the top 10% performers. This is an organizational practice in many companies. Besides performance appraisal purposes, managers must identify and submit an organization plan that has a succession planning subset. Companies then budget and apply resources to the top performers and will then groom them through rewards, coaching, training, and better opportunities. Many companies subscribe to the "people management" theory, in which management time and resources should be focused on the top performers (to retain and to promote them) rather than trying to bring bottom performers up. Again, I'll discuss this more in later sections.

Thinning Within The Herd

Attrition is an opportunity waiting for the right opportunist. Sometimes instead of looking for a promotion, the promotion may come looking for you. Attrition among your co-workers reduces your competition and makes you more visible. Attrition among the upper ranks creates upward opportunities that need to be filled. You do not have control over when and how other employees leave. All you have control over is your performance. In any case, the remaining employees that do perform are rewarded. A large company I worked for used to have a slogan to describe how they weeded out the employees to reach the crème of the crop – "We hire them by the masses, put them in classes, then fire their @$$es (those that didn't perform)." This was pretty close to reality, however crass it may sound, in that the remaining poor or marginal performers, who did not get fired, were often left on their own. Poor performers eventually leave, are fired, or some get really good at getting lost in large corporations. They don't get promoted, but they find ways to stay employed and "fly under the radar", so to speak. One way is to keep changing jobs and departments. It is sad but many companies (and managers) do not have the stomach and/or fortitude to fire a poor performer. It is easier for a manager to shuffle the employee to another department (and fellow Managers….suckers!) When your co-workers leave, a complex dynamic takes place that naturally elevates those remaining to greater visibility.

A natural weeding out process helps managers identify superstars. The budget for salaries and bonuses are spread across fewer employees and promotional opportunities open up and need to be filled with current employees. In high tech companies, many of which are generally both small and fast growing, I saw many secretaries get promoted to Product Managers, Supervisors, and other skilled positions just because they were available. For "normal" corporations, vacancies still open up opportunities. However, you may be thinking, "why would I want to stay on a burning ship if everyone is leaving?" Fair question. There are situations where you should leave. We'll discuss that more later in the book. In my experience, employees don't see or understand promotional possibilities and, thus, miss opportunities. It is still better to be promoted in a dysfunctional corporation, because the learning potential and the bigger job title will help you when you look outside for another job. You may have to tolerate a tough economic business situation, but this too is valuable experience that is virtually priceless.

Job is 8am-5pm, Career is from 5pm-8am; Volunteer for off-hour assignments

When I was a Director, a disappointing observation I had of lower level employees was how many saw work strictly as 8 a.m.-5 p.m., both physically and mentality. These same employees would then complain about how there were no career opportunities or that they did not have the time to develop skills. If those people are your career "competitors," wouldn't you want to get ahead of them? Fact is, there are always more projects or tasks to do than your bosses have resources to work on them. Go to your supervisor and simply ask if (on your own time) you can tackle one of these projects as an employee development exercise. This is part of putting into action any talks you have with your superiors about wanting to advance to a more responsible position in the company. Common business sayings which illustrate these points are "Walk the Talk" and "Put Skin in the Game." It still amazes me how many employees were offended at the thought of putting in their own time to learn new skills that can lead to higher level job opportunities.

Think Beyond Your Immediate Department

Your career potential doesn't stop within your immediate department or group. Ask your supervisor if you can inquire within other departments; perhaps because your career major is elsewhere in the company. If you've made a positive impression on your supervisor, he or she will likely help you with a recommendation or introduction to other departments within the company. Initially, request an informational interview with the other department managers. An informational interview is not a formal interview because there is likely no current job opening. It is used more like a mentorship meeting, whereby you are getting information about that department, various job roles, and what skills are required. In reality, you are fishing for an internship assignment and you are also positioning yourself to be *the* internal candidate, if and when, a position opens up.

More on this topic in the next chapter because it applies to your daily corporate life at all levels of employment within the company.

Novel Concept – Talk to Your Supervisor or Manager

I've alluded to this in earlier. Let me be blunt…it is okay to talk with your supervisor or manager about you. I'm guessing many of you knew this, but did not know what to say or what to ask for. Don't make it more complicated than it needs to be. You want to spend one-on-one time with your manager to get career advice. If you're a top performer, these conversations are easy for both of you. A good manager will offer advice on how you can improve and prepare for the next steps in your career. They will also brainstorm ideas with you and give you exposure and the benefit of their experience. Some examples include getting trained as a backup for them or to be an assistant supervisor, team leader, or just to cover for them in meetings and while they are on vacations.

It's temporary

Young people must have a gene that does not allow them to imagine the future beyond what they can see in front of their face. It must be some evolutionary behavior that protects them from the unknown. Your current situation (and job level) is only temporary. DO NOT take your current situation and extend it into the future. Don't assume that what is will *always* be. Learn to have vision (and faith). Take your current situation and imagine what it can be.

If your early jobs in a corporation are low-level or you don't like the way the corporation operates, don't extrapolate that situation into the future as if nothing will change. With time, changes can and will occur in ways you cannot foresee. You control some of the changes. To illustrate, take a typical Starbucks' barista (no knock on Starbucks or the barista job position). Starbucks does an exceptional job with benefits and work conditions for their baristas, but a barista is the lowest job at Starbucks. As good as the environment and work conditions are at Starbucks, many baristas have the typical hourly worker mentality – they're just there to get a paycheck; it's not where they see themselves years from now.

Why?...One reply is that they cannot see themselves doing the same job or working for the same company years down the road. Probing deeper, it becomes clear that these young people cannot visualize the growth and changes in their role, in the company, nor what they can gain. The result and reality at Starbucks, like many retailers, is a lot of turnover, even at the

Store Manager level. What young people don't realize is there are many promotional opportunities available at Starbucks. With each promotion, you gain valuable experience. It's a different job, and you increase your ability to impact the company, its processes, and its environment.

Key Actions Checklist

☐ Do everything you can to be the top performer at your job function.

☐ Keep up on what is happening with your company, industry, and department so you have an objective view as to whether there are opportunities you should stay for. Don't get caught up with all the gossip and cynicism among fellow co-workers.

☐ Look for off-hour assignments within your department and other departments (with permission from your supervisor or manager, of course).

☐ Request informational interviews with other department leaders.

☐ Schedule meetings with your supervisor or manager to get career feedback and to learn about growth opportunities.

Chapter 7 – Daily Life in the (Corporate) Herd

"Whatever you are, be a good one." ~ Abraham Lincoln

You have your new job. You understand your brand and communications. I am confident you have the foundation to be as good as you can be with your work and your brand. It's no time to be grazing lazily on the corporate pastures. As Mr. Lincoln said, you're all set to do your job well and that's all there is to moving ahead in the corporate world, right? Not quite. To be "good", there's more you need to know and learn.

You'll do okay with what you've learned so far, but the key is to move ahead *soooner*. To do that, you'll need some insight about how the corporate world works *and what additional skills you need to move ahead and do it soooner.* You can take advantage of behind the scenes insights as to how a company works. Some insights are unwritten tribal knowledge you may not recognize if it hits you at work; other stuff is surprisingly common sense.

As you graze and mooove your way around the daily herd life, recognize the following lessons: effective culture, good protocol, and take the initiative to pursue the recommended skills.

What to Do When You Have Good Ideas

When my 25 years old niece was telling me about her new corporate job and their weekly staff meetings, I asked the following question: "When you have a great idea, do you share it with everyone at your staff meetings?" "Of course," she said, "our department is like a family". She was offended and surprised when I replied that I've learned never to share my ideas openly in those settings.

Most of us can't wait to tell anyone who will listen. It's an ego rush. STOP! Don't just blare it out. There is a good time to share your ideas and there are not-so-good times. Recognition for being smart and for being a contributing team member is a great rush for your ego. Control this urge. I strongly recommend you do NOT share your ideas in any group or public setting, such as staff meetings, all-hands meetings, in ad-hoc group settings with fellow employees, or even with employees at lunch. It's tempting; especially at your weekly or monthly department staff meetings.

When your department manager is discussing company and departmental challenges and goals, you are probably bursting at the seams to yell out your ideas. DON'T!!! I know it is hard to keep quiet if you have a good idea or comment in these situations, but fight the urge. It is much more productive and powerful for your career if you share your ideas with your manager directly in a one-on-one, private conversation.

First of all, you'll get her/his undivided attention. Before your meeting, think through your idea, and better yet, document it. You will be able to discuss it with her/him in detail and perhaps even develop the details and implementation with her/him. You will also have an opportunity to share any research you have conducted thoroughly with them, which can increase the chances of your idea turning into something that is actually implemented with the company.

Secondly, you won't create resentment among your peers, which I've seen happen time and time again to the person who "grandstands" in a public setting to "showoff". It can be annoying to others and even embarrassing for you if your idea is not very well developed or maybe even considered ridiculous or frivolous, as it will probably not be well received by your superiors.

Lastly, it is a great excuse to get a meeting with your manager. In sales, you are always looking for a reason to make a sales call/appointment with a potential client (in this case the client just happens to be your manager).

There May Never Be Dumb Questions, But There Is a Dumb Time to Ask One

"There are never dumb questions. The only dumb questions are those that are not asked." I recall this was a very popular saying in school. This is certainly an often-used phrase in seminars, workplace meetings, and formal business gatherings. I absolutely agree with this phrase. We want our kids to be inquisitive. In our adult corporate lives, managers are grateful to have motivated staff members, and one evidence of their motivation is when they make an effort to ask questions. It's not about suppressing a person's desire for discovery or curiosity. So, the idea of asking a question is not a bad thing whatsoever, my issue and recommendation to you is to watch the timing of your questions. A great golden rule I learned from a local musical director is – raise your hand to ask a question only if your question affects all of your fellow cast members.

In other words:

1. Don't waste everyone else's time if you have a selfish question or a selfish need to get attention. On a large musical production, rehearsal time is scarce.

2. Think through things before engaging your mouth. Many people have questions when the answer is right in front of them, or they did not pay attention when it was given, or they can logically deduce it or find it in some other way.

Write down your questions during a meeting while a presenter is making his/her presentation. If your question passes the golden rule above, then ask it. Resist the temptation to show everyone how smart and attentive you are. If your question doesn't pass the golden rule or you're not sure, follow up with the presenter afterward. You can do it in person and the benefit is individual attention. It's also effective to use email or a phone call after the meeting.

Good Ideas Are Only Half of The Puzzle to Getting Ahead

Here's the formula for moving ahead: Good ideas **+ Successful implementation** = moving ahead of the herd. Ideas are "products" you offer to your manager and the corporation. But ideas are not good enough. "Ideas are a dime a dozen" ~ Unknown. Helping to implement the idea, for the benefit for all, completes your true value.

A natural question at this point would be, "What if my manager steals my idea?" You've all seen it in movies or television. Unfortunately, this does actually happen. Again, people can behave badly and some do. I still think this is a risk worth taking, unless you already know your manager is short on integrity. If that is the case, you should look for another department or company to work in or don't share your ideas while you continue to work there. The only reason to share your ideas and help your manager succeed, knowing they are unscrupulous, is for the chance to advance on his or her corporate coattail. The chance of people stealing your idea increases if you blared it out in a group meeting. Remember, it is not the idea that is valuable to the organization; it is the *effective* implementation of that idea (for the benefit of all) that makes an idea valuable. An idea without effective implementation is worthless. Hopefully you will be allowed to implement the idea project; ask for it!

There is a good likelihood your manager will involve you. A manager cannot do everything. Managers have staff because he/she cannot achieve (and implement) all the goals that have been assigned to them. If they could, the unemployment rate would be through the roof and corporations would be comprised entirely of managers.

Brown-Nosers and Yes-People Both Get Ahead

It is sad, but true. I've seen enough examples of both in my career. I will say that being a brown-noser takes a unique talent to do it well and shamelessly. I don't have any advice or insight on how to become a brown-noser: I am not one. Frankly, this style is against my value system. (Google "brown-noser" to get a definition and to find out about its origin because it is somewhat embarrassing to do here). On the other hand, I am advocating that you be a yes-person. A yes-person is someone who will support their manager. Now, I don't mean to imply that you should mindlessly agree with everything your manager does and says, especially if it is illegal or shameless. That's a brown-noser. A yes-person supports their manager by helping them achieve goals. At this stage in your career, I am saying you should say yes and agree with everything your manager says, because I'm assuming you don't have enough experience. If you have input or expertise, it is okay to ask questions and get clarification before engaging in a task or the implementation of projects and policies. But you should not argue with everything your manager says just to show how smart you are or to stroke your ego. Let's be clear on what I mean, we are talking about an early period in your career. As you develop experience and expertise in your career, you can be (and will be expected to be) challenging decisions and ideas and backing up your position with data and alternative solutions. Early in your career, you should agree and support your manager. We will talk more about this in the "Managing Up" chapter.

Tony's Stories

Let's be clear what being a brown-noser is and is not. A brown-noser is someone who says yes to everything her/his supervisor says and wants without any question, shamelessly. Nobody likes to see someone act this way, not even your manager. If you work in a place where this is the culture, look for another company. Sometimes employees don't even realize they're acting like a brown-noser. Managers within these companies, especially high level ones like Directors, VPs, and the President, are viewed and treated like rock stars by employees. There can also be a sort of hero worship and famous person paparazzi atmosphere among employees. You do NOT have to treat or look at your management in this way. It does NOT get you promoted or ahead of the herd (at least not in an ethical way). Very early in my career I worked at a large, old, middle America based company, and there was a summer picnic at our VP's house for a group of us junior sales reps from all over the country visiting corporate headquarters. There was also other corporate staff members invited. The corporate staff members were older, probably in their 30's and 40's. Some reps and staffers were obviously practicing brown-nosers. They would spend all their time trying to talk to the VP while most reps were playing volleyball, eating, talking with each other, or just enjoying the event and weather. Brown-nosers view these events as business-social, rather than social-business. But the most amazing and obvious brown-nosing was when the Senior VP showed up to the party. This gentleman acted out the rock star role to a tee. He came into the backyard where the party was without saying anything to anyone. He sat down at the far end of a table and simply took out a cigarette and held it out. Before you can say "arrogant", three middle-aged staff members tripped over themselves to light the Senior VP's cigarette. I know, to this day, none of those staff members went much further in their careers at that company. There are better, more dignified ways (and better companies to be at) to move your career forward. I knew after seeing that incident, that this particular company (and its culture) was not the place for me.

To Get Ahead in the Herd, Network All the Time Within and Outside of Your Company

When people refer to "networking," they are talking about networking with people outside of your immediate work area. Regardless of how large or small the company, I suggest you network with fellow employees. I'm referring to employees you don't normally or naturally work with as part of your job or departmental function. Specifically I'm referring to the following departments: IT, Facilities, and Finance people. They're the first to know what the company leaders have decided to implement. I'm talking about things like new acquisitions, forced reductions/layoffs, company expansion, selling of the company or division, facility relocation, and so on. Notice I did not include HR in that list? The HR people are naturally secretive about the plans. But in my experience, the people in those other functions are more apt to reveal the plans. By learning of plans sooner, it may serve your career and help you or others through the change in management process that will follow.

It may seem obvious while you're reading this that the Facilities people would know of any plans that involved facilities. I would venture to say that in your daily workings, you never really thought about this. If you did, you would have friends in Facilities at this moment. Do you? My bet is you don't. Well, you should. The Facilities department is engaged in the early planning stages of any business expansion or contraction and relocation. A great way to network with people in other parts of the corporation is to participate in company social events, such as company softball teams, charity events, even company choirs (which I did when I was at Hewlett-Packard, even though I didn't know how to carry a tune...I learned something about singing and reading music from the experience besides meeting people in other functions of what was then still a very large company).

Tony's Stories

When I was at Sun Microsystems, I knew nearly a year in advance about a pending move of the entire Customer Service group (2,000) people from Northern California to Boulder, Colorado. I used that information to secure a job and location of my own choice because I did not want to move to Colorado. In every case I was involved in an acquisition, the acquiring company I was a member of told the target companies that everything would stay the same, including their facility. However, I learned in advance from my Facilities contacts that the executives had plans to close or relocate the targeted companies. Whenever there are decisions about people, the IT people are the first to know because they have to organize network access or plan for the installation or reduction of networks. The Finance Department is also involved in just about every plan because they are modeling the various options for analysis.

Hard and Soft skills You Need That You Did Not Learn in College

Sure, you've spent years in college and probably spent time as an intern and held jobs all throughout high school and college. You may even be a mid-career person with experience in the corporate world. You have skills. The questions is: do you have ***all the skills*** to get ahead in the corporate world? I am confident that you have *not* developed the necessary hard and soft skills that will help you get ahead in the corporate herd, sooner. How do I know this? Because they're not typically taught. Where in your life have you learned the following:

- to be an effective presenter

- to really understand corporate finance and departmental budgeting

- to sell

- a variety of other soft skills including interpersonal communications, leadership, active listening, etc.

Although these skills can be learned early on, such as during college or sooner, I doubt most people can and will learn them at that stage, if ever. They are not in any curriculum or requirements. Rarely does someone assign you to learn these skills. Even if you knew about them, you probably were not motivated or didn't see the need. That's all fine because you had a lot of foundational things to learn. Now you're in your 20's or 30's and it's high time that you learn and develop these vital skills.

In the corporate world, managers refer to an employee as having hard skills and soft skills. Hard skills are the specific knowledge or ability to perform the job in a satisfactory manner. Hard skills can be learned. Examples of hard skills include writing, programming, operating a folk lift, using Microsoft Excel, etc. Hard skills are the minimum criteria managers and corporations look for in an employee. It's a "me too" item, meaning that everyone must have an acceptable level of that skill to qualify. Again, the good news is that hard skills can be learned. You can take a class, read a book, or have someone teach them to you.

Soft skills are those that are difficult to learn even if they can be taught. Soft skills are more of art than a science. You will likely be good at some soft skills and not as natural with others. Soft skills require more experience than hard skills to master. Examples of soft skills include: attitude, creativity, friendliness, personality traits, interpersonal interactions, dependability, conscientiousness, leadership, coaching and mentoring, motivating others, active listening, negotiations, and many more.

Most manager say if they had to, or given a choice between qualified candidates, they would hire for soft skills even if the candidate does not have the hard skills. Managers and their companies can teach the hard skills, not soft skills. Soft skills cannot be easily learned, but don't despair because I've seen people improve soft skills, and one component of this is to recognize you have a need to improve. The other component needed to improve a soft skill is the motivation to actually do it.

Here are three essential ones you should work on early in your career:

Be a Great Presenter

There are not many hard skills I will stress in this book as being important to your corporate career, but one of them is to be a good presenter. I know, you hated the communications class in college and you dread public speaking. You better get over it! Presentation skills will help you project a confident, professional, knowledgeable presence, even in small gatherings. Of all people, I dreaded presenting. I was not born with this skill so I needed to learn and practice this skill. Early in my career, I was awful. Maybe it was genetic. Maybe many young people have the same problem. I didn't know either way. Looking back, I'm embarrassed to recall how geeky I looked, how fast and jittery I spoke, and how I did not enunciate well. In short, I don't believe people had a very high professional opinion of me. It was tough enough, as an Asian, to project maturity because we are ethnically younger looking compared to the image people have of a professional in the corporate world. Nevertheless, I didn't know this. Nobody told me. And I didn't even know the questions to ask to gain knowledge of this skill.

Two things finally alerted me to this handicap:

- At Apple Computer, we had a required presentation class for everyone in my department. We had to present in the class to fellow classmates. You would think that would provide some comfort, but it was nerve-racking. The real shock came at the end of the class when we were videotaped and the instructor spent private one-on-one time with each of us to provide valuable feedback. Want to be humbled? Try a video analysis exercise and you will be. Fact is – we don't learn to be good presenters. It is not a natural trait. From what I've seen, this skill is not a common gene in our DNA makeup.

- The second time that helped to reinforce the need for me to work on becoming a better presenter was also when I was at Apple Computer. I learned that John Sculley, President and CEO of Pepsi who came to Apple to become President and CEO, had a coach to help him improve his presentation skills. He was not very good. I saw him present a lot and so I was (and wasn't) surprised he had a private coach. He presented at company all-hands meetings. He presented at MacWorld and the Developer's Conference, and many, many other conferences Apple participated in or sponsored. It was painful and sort of embarrassing to watch him. Granted, technology was not his cup of tea, so perhaps he was simply nervous because he was not comfortable with the subject. After all, he spent his entire career at Pepsi, a sugar water company, and there's not much technology involved in that product aside from the bottling process. At Apple, he had to talk about the vision of personal computing, bits and bytes, integrated circuit speed, and stuff that hadn't even been invented yet. He had to and did learn facts and concepts, such as the computer and technology stuff, pretty quickly, but he needed help with the one hard skill that I found I was missing too – presentation skills. You would think a guy who was President and CEO of Pepsi, a multi-billion dollar corporation, would have had lots of practice, right? Well, apparently he didn't and was able to get around this issue all this time. However, he practiced, got coaching, and soon he improved his presentation skills 300%.

What is the lesson to learn here? Well, you too can learn and practice public speaking and how to make good, effective and impressive presentations. Join a local Toastmasters club. Get yourself videotaped and work on being smooth, practice good posture, proper gestures, learn to use notes, and improve your appearance. Get someone to give good, honest, tough-love feedback. For me, that person was my wife. I knew her constructive criticism was just that, constructive. It wasn't a personal attack. She helped me immensely with my enunciation, pace of speech, eye contact, and she pushed me to practice, practice, practice.

Part of being a good presenter has to do with the content, not just the presentation itself. It's one thing to be a good presenter, but you will still not be as effective if you do not present your material in an organized and convincing manner. It would be sort of like making a movie with the latest special effects, lighting, audio, and music track, but the movie has a terrible script and it's edited poorly. A Senior VP gave me an invaluable tip that I will share with you. He gave me a book that apparently all consultants consider a must-read, *The Pyramid Principle*, by Barbara Minto. Since the purpose of most presentations is to convince people of something, such as a proposal or position, this book teaches a useful, structured approach to organizing the content to help you achieve approval or support for your purpose. I found Ms. Minto's approach very useful for proposal presentations. For more routine presentations, such as operational reviews and status reports, another Senior VP taught me a useful approach that is a short cut way of thinking in preparing the presentation. He called it "story telling." What is the story you want tell? Everything is great and here's how we did it and the results? Or, things didn't go as plan, and here's why and what we're going to do about it. There's your structure. Now just fill in all of the details.

Know the Numbers of Corporate Finance

You're wondering, "Why do I need to learn Finance? I'm a _____(fill in the blank with any major other than Finance) major." Wrong my Padawan (An apprentice of a Jedi Master – yes, I am a big Star Wars fan). I thought the same thing early in my career. My undergraduate degree was in Marketing with an Associates degree in Electronics. When I went back to school to get my MBA, I focused on Finance because I saw that effective corporate leaders had a deep understanding of finance. They knew the numbers, and I am not talking about accounting. There is a marked difference between Accounting and Finance. Accounting is simply the tracking of business transactions and journal entries. Finance is looking at the compilation of those transactions in the form of the Profit/Loss Statements and the Balance Sheet. Moreover, finance involves the analysis of the numbers and the cause and effect of the numbers.

As I progressed in my career, I found that my finance knowledge was inadequate. It was partly due to the poor education I had received in college; it was also a lack of motivation. Okay, maybe it was more the latter. Numbers and analyzing them did not excite me. If I enjoyed it, I would have majored in Accounting or Finance; at least that was my thinking at the time. I'm sure many of you reading this can admit the same thing. Together, the result ended in moments at executive operations meetings where I was clueless as to what was happening in the overall business, while peers and superiors around me were talking about it like they were playing fantasy baseball, discussing the stats and interpreting the possible causes from the background data. They were on top of just a sample of the following: monthly and quarterly results, what it was against year-over-year, quarter over quarter, month over month, the top line number, by product line, gross margin, cost of goods sold, SG&A (sales and general administration expenses), EBITA (pronounced *ee-ba-ta*; Earnings Before Interest, Taxes, and Amortization), and net profit. The moral of the story is – learn finance in general and be comfortable with the financial scorecard of your department and of the overall company business.

Selling

You're in sales. Most of you are saying to yourself right now, "No I'm not! Yuck, who wants to be a salesperson?" It's unfortunate that the sales profession has such a stigma attached to it, which is mostly proliferated by extreme examples of hard-selling characters. Our culture has stereotyped the over-the-top extrovert car salesperson hovering over you on the car lot and the smooth talking insurance salesperson. Most sales positions are not so extreme. Nevertheless, you should be using some of the sales techniques because you are selling all the time, either professionally or personally. Selling occurs more often than you would imagine. Any interaction with a fellow human being involves "selling". It's just not called selling. However, words like "persuasion, motivation, influence, leadership, evangelize, induce, sway, control, pressure, transform" and so on are all forms of "selling" someone on something. You're selling yourself (a.k.a. your brand). You're selling ideas. You're selling to customers. You're selling to vendors. You are selling when you are persuading fellow employees and friends to support your cause or even to someplace that you'd like to go for lunch. Selling skills have parallels to successful negotiations.

Three key elements to effective selling:

1. **Identify the hot buttons.** A hot button is a sales terms to describe those features and benefits that will persuade a person or organization to "buy" into what you are offering or proposing. You're probably thinking the primary hot button is usually price. Not true. Price can be a primary factor, but in most cases there are other factors, such as features, convenience, reputation, etc. Sales people are trained to identify the hot buttons, then focus on the features and benefits that match up.

2. **Handling objections.** Effective probing is what separates the good sales people from the not-so-good ones. People don't just tell you what their buying hot buttons are or why they won't buy. Even if you ask, what they tell you is not reliable as the "truth". Many people don't know what they don't know. There may be features and benefits they did not think of that will matter. The key to effective probing is uncovering objections. When a person has objections, they are essentially highlighting a hot button. Once the objection(s) are uncovered, you can address them.

3. **Go for the close.** When you have someone convinced, secure it. In sales, it's called "close for the order". You don't need to preach to the converted. When the person is nodding their head or they actually say something like, "I like your idea," they are telling you they support your plan. After you confirm their

support, move on to discussing the mechanics of the purchase or the implementation.

Always be ready to answer the silent question in a potential customer's mind: the "so what?" or "what's in it for me?". As long as the potential customer has objections, you have not translated a feature into a benefit that is important to the customer. Here's a real life example – selling someone a hybrid car. Hybrid cars are hot, but people still need to be convinced. A hybrid car is not a slam-dunk purchase decision. A small percentage of people who are very technical might buy the car, regardless of the price, simply because they like the technology. Chances are you will have to tell people what the price benefits are along with other benefits, depending upon their hot button – lower maintenance cost, lower fuel cost from less gasoline usage, good for the environment because of reduced emissions, music sounds better because the car is quieter, fewer stops for refills because the car has a longer range, and so on. The same process can be used for communicating (selling) your messages to your staff, to senior management, etc. There are great books, seminars, and information on the Internet about sales techniques. Go learn this skill as soon as you can.

Don't Leave Dead Bodies

Getting the job done and getting it done right are two different things. "Getting the job done doesn't count if it's not done right". This was one of the sayings from a General Manager I reported to in reference to achieving your goals and getting credit for it. He said that just because you hit (or exceed) your goals, it doesn't count if you accomplished it through methods that are illegal at worst, and at best, got everyone around you pissed off. Having co-workers upset or irritated in the wake of your work is the proverbial "dead bodies." The illegal part is easy to understand. Laws are black and white. You either take a bribe or you don't. The other "right ways" are subjective and gray. The point my General Manager was trying to make was – you need to go about your business adhering to a set of business and cultural values and moral standards. Many of the values are grounded in humanity. Non-business people would say these values are common courtesy and common sense. It's all of the above. Some companies put values in writing. A few companies include values in a person's annual performance review.

Here is a sampling:

- Win-win

- Teamwork

- Credit where credit is due

- Professionalism

- Customer first

- Integrity

- Financial success

- Respect others

We've discussed poor behavior in people in earlier sections and we'll have more later in the book. This is a tricky subject. What's "right" to some is not so "right" to others. People working in groups create many dynamics. It is not my place here to make black and white what is generally many shades of gray when it comes to human behavior and human interaction. I will direct you to the following perspectives so you can decide for yourself:

1. What does your upbringing and your heart tell you?

2. What is your manager's philosophy?

3. What is your company's or industry's culture and practices?

If You Get the Boss From Hell, No Amount of Money Is Worth It

I used to hear about the Boss from Hell (BFH) through news articles and magazine stories. I didn't believe they actually existed. Those stories about the psychotic boss that yells at people or gives absurd orders sounded like it only happened in movies. I've never seen or had a boss like this. It may happen, but I think these physical behaviors would not be tolerated into today's policy-laden work environment. The type of BFH who can operate undetected uses psychological weapons, not physical ones. They make your life miserable in a subtler and far less visible way, like being condescending and critical. You never seem to do anything good enough, no matter how much instruction you get from them. They are very anal and detail oriented. They demand to know everything you are doing, when, how, and why. They want weekly status reports and they pick at every report you turn in including the report format, even though *they* gave you the format to use.

What should you do if you are in this situation? Do what I did…GET OUT! Get another job in another department and if you cannot, get out of the company as soon as possible.

There is no magic solution for this situation. You can't change the person. Don't report your situation to HR. The BFH is not breaking any laws. They are not committing sexual or any defined harassment (racial, gender, profane, sarcastic, or physical). There is no law or policy against a boss who is simply being really, really tough and detailed. There is no law against a boss who wants you to rewrite the report over and over again until it meets their standard. And don't think you can rally fellow employees to somehow help to overthrow the BFH. I was in a situation once where a group of employees tried this and the "rebel leader" ended up getting fired and the boss blackballed anyone associated. Bottom line, you are not going to get the BFH moved, fired, or reprimanded.

The BFH's bosses don't do anything because they don't see or experience what you do; and in reality, they don't care. They are unable to "put the shoe on the other foot" and probably wouldn't be willing to change their methods even if they could. Like all bosses, they only care that the goals they issued are achieved – even at the expense of bad morale. A short word about employee morale – don't believe what upper management says about how important employees morale is to them, they really don't care! The conventional wisdom is that happy employees are more productive and help preserve customers and increase sales. This might be true, but it is very difficult to make a direct correlation. The real measure is whether goals are achieved. I've never seen or heard of a manager or executive with a goal to achieve some level of employee morale. I've seen attempts at making employee retention a goal, but this is not common. It's really a shame because studies have shown over and over again that an employee's work satisfaction is most directly affected by their immediate supervisor and not by any larger factors, such as company policies, products, industry or competitors.

Tony's Stories

My Boss from Hell (BFH) never smiled or engaged in small talk with me. The constant belittling and berating took its toll on me. Prior to working for the BFH, I had always been successful and confident. I was a director level executive at a Fortune 100 company. I thought to myself, "How did I suddenly become incompetent?" After six months with the

BFH, I questioned my self-worth. All those physical stress symptoms you read about began happening to me. I couldn't sleep. I didn't want to get out of bed to go to work. I feared any phone calls and emails from my BFH. I tried to avoid the BFH at all costs. My saving grace was learning from fellow peers who were also going through similar trials with the BFH.

In my case and to this point, my BFH acted completely different with his superiors and with people outside our department. His superiors commented on how funny he was. Female employees in other departments commented on how friendly he was and how he liked to joked around with them. He was civilized and quite a host at the holiday party he threw at his house. He had a very nice family. But come Monday at the department staff meeting, watch out!

Preparing For The Annual Performance Review

Your daily herd life will quickly turn from days to a year. Before you know it your new job is not so new and you're about to be given your first formal performance review.

Some people treat annual performance reviews like an annual trip to the dentist. This annual event can be like a painful drilling into your shortcomings and areas requiring improvement. The performance review can also be something you enjoy because it is an affirmation of your stellar performance (and the deserved salary merit increase also makes it feel pretty good, as well). I absolutely looked forward to it, even though my bosses always had suggestions for improvement; I still thought the constructive criticism was positive. You should too. The trick is to get feedback and assessment throughout the year from your manager. The actual mechanics do not have to be formal. You meet with your manager regularly throughout the year. If he/she does not schedule it, you should request occasional one-on-ones. Just ask your manager how he/she thinks you are performing. If you want to structure the feedback, ask your manager how you are doing against your goals and run down the goals for him or her. And if you do this correctly, you will give him BOTH your goal and your current performance to goal. If he has a different assessment, you can get it cleared up well before the annual performance review event. In short, there should NEVER be a surprise at the annual event.

Let's review the mechanics of an annual performance review from the perspective of the manager and how you can help to make an easier less painful process for all involved. The following are the steps a manager must do to prepare for the actual face-to-face performance review meeting:

At the beginning of the year, your manager will give you your goals. Depending upon the position and department function, you may have an opportunity to "negotiate" the goals. The more your goals are quantifiable, the better. Note: many managers are not experts at goal definition, so don't assume your goals are perfect and non-negotiable. A good manager will develop **SMART goals** (<u>s</u>pecific, <u>m</u>easurable, <u>a</u>ttainable, <u>r</u>ealistic, <u>t</u>imely). And if your manager is not "smart" enough to give you SMART goals, help him/her out because this will actually help you out. An example of a "dumb" goal – "improve the turnaround time for repairing the XYZ product". What makes this a dumb goal? Well, you spend a year improving the turnaround from 45 days to 44 days. Strictly speaking, you achieved the stated goal, but your competitor's turnaround time is 30 days. Your achievement did not make your company competitive. A SMART goal would be – "In 6 months, decrease the maximum repair turnaround time for XYZ product to 40 days and in one year down to 30 days". This goal statement is more specific because it is timely and measurable. It's always a good idea to be detailed and specific when stating your goals for performance reviews. You also need to discuss what you need to achieve the results and your manager must decide what results they will see if they do not approve and provide the necessary resources.

After the new review year, managers must write their assessment of your performance for last year. If your corporation's process requires the manager to obtain feedback from others in the company (such as with 180 and 360 degree feedback processes), the manager has to wait for the feedback and then incorporate it into their assessment. Some corporations have applications to help everyone reduce the amount of writing and collaboration involved in this process. In any case, this process is tremendously taxing on everyone, especially on managers.

Your manager will give you his/her assessment to review so you have a chance to agree or disagree with his/her assessment and to provide any counter arguments and support if you disagree. You should be keeping track of your performance against your goals throughout the year, so that you will have all the data supporting your performance. This is more difficult when your goal(s) is not quantifiable.

You return the assessment with your input. Your manager will schedule a face-to-face meeting with you to go over the review and typically tell you what your salary increase for the New Year will be.

At the face-to-face meeting, the manager will verbalize what he/she wrote in the assessment. He/she may elaborate on the areas of improvement if you have questions. You should use this time to help your manager develop an improvement plan. For example, you've been told to improve your interpersonal skills. If you have ideas or suggestions, such as a class or book, ask your manager if he/she would put that in the plan. Many managers are so overwhelmed by logistics and mechanics of all the reviews they have to write, and the critical nature of the reviews, that they don't even develop good, effective improvement plans.

As usual, there are exceptions depending on your position and the departmental functions. With some large, lower level function departments this process is not followed to this detail and is much more abbreviated and impersonal. The basic insight and suggestions are still useful for you to use whenever and wherever possible with your manager.

Old Cows Can't Learn New Tricks (old Cows Can Learn New Tricks, But It's Harder.)

It might be a bit early to be thinking about 5 years at any job or company. I'm sure you did not think about your senior year when you were trying to register for your first semester of college. Before you know it, you're a Senior. Where did the fours years go? This happens with your job too. Before you know it, you've been there 5 years. How do you stay enthusiastic and fresh? Well, you need to be aware early on what changes occur with tenure at any organization; and how to counteract the changes so they do not undermine your potential to get ahead of the herd. Your image or brand in college was not tied to your ability to advance and complete your degree. In the corporate world, tenure in a company can instill poor practices and certain mind-sets, which in turn can significantly affect your brand negatively.

Here are ways to ways to counteract the effects of tenure:

Change seats on the bus

I used to tell my top employees that they should change jobs, either sideways or upward, within 3-5 years to avoid the risk of getting stale in their job and their career. In fact, I put this into their annual job performance evaluation and as part of their career path planning. Best way to get jobs in different functional areas of a corporation? Change jobs even if it's a lateral move. We will talk more in other sections about

72

changing buses (corporations) but one reason to do so is to broaden your experience.

Be open and inquisitive (remember earlier discussions about connecting the dots?)

And here's that theme again. Make no mistake; this theme goes beyond your job. The dots do connect even if they are not immediately obvious. Drive to become a modern day Renaissance person. In the mid-1970's, there were many business articles and books saying workers get ahead by specializing. I noticed that was a half-truth. It was helpful in the earlier career stages, but to get into the leadership level, a generalist advanced. You will hear this in corporate world – companies are looking for top employees to act like mini-general managers, managing their little positions as if they are the CEO of that position. This is difficult to do if you don't have a broad understanding.

Broaden your skills and knowledge

Have you heard about the person who has been a secretary for 10 years and wondered why no one will consider her/him for a Junior Project manager position (or some other job growth position?) I heard similar situations like this a number of times. Sadly, the secretary did not know the answer. Part of that answer was that she or he got comfortable in their job and never developed the skills or made any preparation to be qualified for another job. There is no excuse because, thanks to the Internet, knowledge is available in so many forms. I remember when one of my bosses, the Senior VP, was about to inherit a sales team and I was pitching him on letting me start an Inside Sales team. It turned out that he had no sales experience, but over one weekend he had read several books and Internet articles on the art of selling. He was a great example of a person who continually evolved his knowledge base. He wasn't going to be an expert overnight, but he armed himself with a better grasp of the topic and he learned enough to bring in enough expertise to accomplish the goals and task. In short, he was (and still is) a model of the ever-evolving and highly effective corporate superstar.

Get outside your department and company

I once had a VP that said, "If you want to get ahead, you have to work two shifts – 9am-5pm in your job and 5pm-9am on your career". He was basically encouraging us to get outside our present job duties and make the personal investment to better ourselves. Go to trade shows and conferences if you can directly justify it, depending upon your position or department. Find out if your marketing department participates in trade shows and ask if you can help out in the booth, using your vacation time if necessary. Most people I knew in marketing got pretty tired of working trade shows. I always found tradeshows, conferences, and classes outside of the physical work environment to be extremely useful in meeting new people, getting ideas, and learning something that I can then apply at work. The simple act of being away from the office allowed my brain to think of new things and new approaches to current problems that I could not easily solve due to the daily pressures at work. Spend time reading about other businesses, people, what they're doing, etc. Sift through progressive magazines like Wired, Business 2.0, and Harvard Business Review. Join local business associations, such as American Asian Marketing Association, Clean Tech Consortium, Product Development & Management Associations, Toast Masters, etc. Social networks, such as Meetup.com, on the Internet are becoming effective resources for physical business and non-business gatherings.

Key Actions Checklist

- ☐ Write down your ideas. Do your research to flush out the idea and alternative solutions. Then set up a time to go over them with your manager.

- ☐ Continue practicing networking. Shift focus to those in your network who can advise you about career path and people in your industry.

- ☐ Take presentation classes. Join Toast Masters. Read the book *The Pyramid Principle*, by Barbara Minto. Practice.

- ☐ Take a corporate finance class. Ask your manager to walk you through the company/division budget and financial results. Ask to sit through a finance review (generally happens every quarter).

- ☐ Take sales training. Read sales books. Ride shotgun with a company sales rep.

- ☐ Maintain on-going notes of accomplishments so you don't have to recall them months later at the annual performance review.

- ☐ Learn new functions and tasks. Keep educated through conferences, seminars, and periodicals.

Chapter 8 – Managing Up

"By working faithfully eight hours a day you may eventually get to be boss and work twelve hours a day." ~ Robert Frost

The concept of managing up is one of the most profound that I have learned. As the term implies, "Managing Up" is about how you work with people who have seniority over you in the corporate hierarchy. It is about the hard, cold reality of what your first and most important responsibility is within a corporation. Your most important responsibility is NOT achieving your goals; it is NOT doing a good job; it is NOT being a good employee; and it is NOT branding yourself. Your first and most important responsibility is to help your manager succeed.

I realize this is confusing. If you do a good job and accomplish your professional goal, by default your manager will succeed, right? To some degree, yes, but I am talking about going much deeper, so that you will achieve beyond yourself. I am talking about a different perspective that reveals better ways for you to approach your job. Let me explain.

Up to this point, we've been talking about managing yourself and the daily corporate life of working with others. Later in this book we'll talk about managing down. Your focus at this point in your career, and in this book, is to learn how to "manage up."

So how do you manage up? By realizing that your foremost role is to make your manager successful, and thinking beyond yourself. It's a state of mind. You do not wait for your manager to hand you goals and instructions. Instead, you proactively look at your manager's goals, and determine how to help him achieve those goals. Your goals need to roll up into your manager's goals, just as your Manager's goals roll up into the Director's goals, whose goals roll up into the VP's goals, whose goals roll up into the company's goals. I worked at only one company where this very useful goal alignment concept was shared with employees.

When you are proactively working to support your manager's goals, you will automatically think about information your manager needs, information that will help your manager prepare status meetings with management. You will naturally start to think like your manager. You will anticipate things. You will become familiar with your manager's role and what he needs. You will experience more open and productive communication with your manager and, in turn, your working relationship will become collaborative, rather than boss-to-subordinate. I'll stress it again – you need to proactively support your manager's goals and anticipate what your manager needs. Managers notice this proactive behavior among staff members. They notice it because…well, because it's very rare.

If you learn to manage up, it will not only help your manager succeed, it will also help you succeed, too. When you are proactive in managing up, you become more comfortable with upper level protocols, communications, expectations, and problem solving; and you become less anxious about being around senior leaders.

Here are my Managing Up Golden Rules:

Determine Your Manager's Operating System (Personal Style)

First and foremost, you need to determine your manager's operating system. In computer terms, an operating system is the set of rules, processes, and procedures that dictate how components and software work together. Being a tech guy, I easily see the metaphor of an operating system representing the interaction between a manager and staff members. A manager's operating system may include rules for items such as:

- How often does your manager want to meet with you/your team?

- Where does your manager want to meet?

- What method does your manager prefer for receiving information and updates? Does he/she prefer email, cell phone, voicemail, drop into office?

- Does she/he have an open door policy?

- What process does she/he prefer for scheduling their time? Do they have someone manage their calendar?

- Does she/he want regular activity reports? If so, what format?

- Which actions require your manager's approval? Which spending levels require your manager's signature?

You need to identify the operating system (personal style) of your manager. Everyone has different preferences. I used to tell my staff that I hated voicemail because I was usually not in a position to take notes while listening to voicemail. I prefer email, text, or a face-to-face meeting. The current use of smartphones greatly helps me because now I can easily access all my emails, texts, documents, calendar events...and yes, I can even listen to voicemails.

Ask your manager to list their preferences on communicating and things involved in the daily routine. Many managers won't share this information unless they are asked. Perhaps many haven't even thought about it, but of the many people I've worked for, only one discussed their personal preferences with me. And not coincidentally, I think this understanding was a key factor in our successful working relationship.

Note: Generally a manager's operating system is not up for negotiations. Operating system parameters are dictated by the boss. After all, the boss' needs come first and foremost.

Don't let your manager get blindsided; no surprises

The golden rule of "no surprises" applies all the way up the corporate pyramid to the corporate shareholders. Have you noticed that when a company reports earnings that are better than expected, the company's stock price can get beaten down by Wall Street analysts? Why? They were surprised. To the analysts, the company's Board of Directors, and the shareholders, surprises indicate that the management team didn't have a good handle on their business operations.

One way you can help your manager succeed is to protect him from looking bad when dealing with peers and superiors. To do this, make sure your manager has all the information needed regarding project status, organizational situations, and even information considered gossip. The bottom line is to eliminate surprises and give your manager time to digest and deal with the information you provide. The worst thing that can happen to your manager is to be surprised in a public setting, also known as being "blindsided."

Routine status updates, given with your manager's personal preference in mind, (adjusted to your manager's personal style) will help your manager to do his job better. However, there are often so many things going on, that information relayed in "real time" truly needs to be tailored to your manager's personal style. Therefore, establish how your manager prefers to see text and email messages.

Let Your Manager Know About Good News, But Bad News Even Sooner

When things are going well or a goal is achieved, people can't wait to tell their Manager and everyone else around them. That's the case outside of work, too. It's human nature to get excited about positive news, while delaying and even avoiding bad news. Just don't do this in the corporate world! A good manager wants to know about a bad situation as soon as possible. This allows for enough time to solve it, mitigate it, minimize the impact, warn others, or get more resources involved, etc.

Most young employees (and some seasoned ones) think the corporate world expects them to deal with problems on their own. This has been portrayed in movies depicting the person heroically saving the company. This is absolutely not the case in real corporate life. The #1 rule of "no surprises" means that you should never get in a position to solve problems by yourself.

8-Minute Rule

Studies have shown that at each progressing level of management, managers have less and less time to spend on any one topic. [example: *The Effective Executive*, by Peter F. Drucker]. Most researchers agree that, depending upon the management level; the average amount of time spent on any one topic is in minutes. From my experience, managers get antsy after 10 minutes. They want to condense everything and get to the point. Therefore, eight minutes is a good target. Never expect your manager to devote more than eight minutes to any one topic.

To Manage Up effectively, you need to be empathetic to your manager's chaotic schedule and urgent time demands. You need to put information into concise packages for your manager. You should also get to know your manager's personality type. Is he/she a type A? Does he/she have adult ADD (attention deficit disorder)? Knowing this will help you to determine the best way to present information to your manager.

When you have the opportunity to provide information to your manager, state the situation, issue, impact and your recommended solutions, alternative and contingencies all within eight minutes. After this, give your manager all the supporting details, such as reports, or data needed to work on the problem.

DO NOT simply forward emails to your manager. Countless times, staff members just forward emails or drop off long documents, expecting their boss to read through all the information to get to the core issue. This leaves the boss uninformed and forced to guess at what the bottom line is. Worse yet, the manager is wondering if any action is required. Is there an issue or not? Do not make this mistake! Summarize the situation in a way that your manager can quickly and easily understand. Don't ever make them sort through data to find the pieces of information that you feel are pertinent.

Present your information in the most concise format possible. Short paragraphs, bullet points and a brief outline form work best. Think through how to concisely and effectively communicate the information to help your manager save time. Believe me, by making the effort to communicate efficiently, you are "managing up" and demonstrating your value.

Exception-Basis

The corporate world operates on an Exception-basis. This means that managers spend 20% of their time on non-problems or things that are running smoothly, and 80% of their time solving problems or those exceptions that are making things difficult. Once you understand this, you'll learn to tailor your information into easily digested information that quickly states, identifies and recommends solutions.

Most organizations use Dashboard or Signal Light reports to simplify status communication and highlight exceptions. In these reports, exceptions are colored in red to indicate areas that require damage control. Items in green are under control and are going as planned. Items in yellow are experiencing some trouble (one or more established boundaries, such as cost or schedule, have been exceeded). Most of the time spent in-status meetings is devoted to addressing the exceptions (red items on the Dashboard or red lights on the Signal Light report.)

Monthly Status Dashboard - Sept 2012				
Tasks/Initiatives	Summary	Target	Actual	Corrective Measures
Response Time	✓	0:30	0:27	
Avg Talk Time	✗	4:00	4:45	Additional Training
Customer Satisfaction	✓	4.0	4.3	
New software tool go-live	◑	9/1/2012	10/1/2012	Overtime for developers
Turnover - Cust Serv Reps	✓	2	0	
Complete New Product Training	◑	9/15/2012	9/22/2012	Product Mgr to schedule additional sessions

Expect, Encourage, Welcome Your Manager's Devil's Advocates

Managing Up requires you to anticipate your manager's questions. It is only over time and experience that you will learn to do this. Most managers have learned to post their questions in a Devil's Advocate style. Understand that this is not a personal attack, but a way to look objectively at a problem and try to discover innovative solutions to problems. Playing the devil's advocate is to question a presented approach or solution, and to argue how another approach could work. You can learn from this.

The devil's advocate approach is a manager's short cut for reviewing and testing a proposal from a staff member to see if it is bulletproof. When your manager is playing devil's advocate, some of his questions and suggestions will be completely hair-brained and useless. But I have observed that usually 50% of the time, their comments will be head-on and thought provoking.

You can anticipate your manager's questions and prepare for them prior to meeting with your manager. Test-drive your proposal with at least three people. Choose one advocate, one middle-of-the-road advocate, and one devil's advocate (someone who you know will rip holes through your ideas). This method will provide various perspectives that you can use to make adjustments to your proposal before you present them to your manager.

Early in my career, I noticed that many employees are so attached to an idea that they become very defensive when alternative approaches were suggested to them. A manager's role is to force open the status quo and use free form thinking to make sure all of the bases are covered. His questions are probably the ones he anticipated being asked when he has to report higher up the chain of command. So when you find that your manager is playing the devil's advocate with you, rather than defending your position, take the opposite tactic: try to make the alternative approaches work, while also identifying the hurdles that must be overcome.

Learn to appreciate what you can gain from your manager's devil's advocate approach. At the very least, a devil's advocate session with your manager will force you to review new positions, review your own position, and accept or deny a better approach. That's how projects and staff members improve.

The devil's advocate approach is a little bit of tough-love, but as long as you realize the approach is not a personal attack, you will quickly understand its value. You will also learn to play devil's advocate in advance, thereby anticipating your manager's questions. This can help you both succeed at finding the best solution in any given situation.

A Final Word

As you progress in the corporate world, you will Manage Up for the rest of your corporate life. Don't believe that it "is lonely at the top." It isn't. Even the CEO reports to someone. When you become a manager, (notice I didn't say "if") teach your staff the concept of Managing Up and help them in applying the advice presented in this chapter. This concept is too valuable to hide or keep to yourself. When you share this concept, you are improving your management style by surrounding yourself with a staff of effective business communicators who will eventually become managers and leaders (and maybe one day, they will, in turn, point to you as one of their best role models.).

Key Actions Checklist

☐ Ask your manager to describe his personal operating system or work style.

☐ Ask your manager to go over his goals with you and, if possible, talk about how those goals align with the larger corporate goals.

☐ Be sure you never let your manager get blind-sided! Always report bad news as soon as possible.

☐ Remember the 8-minute rule. Always prepare for concise communication before meeting with your manager.

☐ Understand Exception reporting; exceptions usually get all the attention.

☐ Welcome your manager's devil's advocate position; learn from it and use it to improve your proposals before you present them to your manager.

Chapter 9 – So you want to be a manager? Really?

"One of the most important tasks of a manager is to eliminate his people's excuses for failure." ~ Robert Townsend

Why do you want to be a manager?

I know this is a rhetorical question and maybe the answer is so obvious that it is a silly question to ask. The simple and obvious answer is – to make more money. Corporate workers, especially younger workers, equate being a manager with getting ahead, and earning a higher salary. This is not always the case, but it is darn close.

All of the above are good motivators, but they are just the dessert after you achieve the manager position. A higher salary and bigger title do not provide the proper context for aspiring managers, as to the "how" and "what" a manager is, in order to prepare themselves to get a manager job or promotion. Sadly, the desire to make more money is NOT a good guideline for people who want to become a manager. Money is a good motivator to want to get ahead, but that doesn't showcase what skills and qualifications are needed to move ahead, starting with being a manager. What I mean is that a person's desire to make more money does not translate into useful actions to becoming a manager. You cannot go into your manager's office and ask for a promotion simply because your reason is to "make more money." You have to determine what the qualifications are to be a manager of whatever department or function you so choose, and then strive to meet them. You also must have genuine desire or passion to perform the tasks of a manager. How are you going to have passion for the tasks if you have no idea what a manager's REAL responsibilities are? Managers don't earn the "big bucks" for doing absolutely nothing.

People often think that they want to be a manager, but know very little about what is required to fulfill the role successfully. During interviews and mentoring sessions, when I have asked candidates and staff members what their career goals are, they would answer, "I want to be a manager." Then I would ask the proverbial test question, "*Why* do you want to be a manager, besides the higher pay?" I always heard the same responses: 1) "I like working with people" or, 2) "I like leading others" or 3) "I like to be in charge." Most people have no idea what a manager's real role is. It is not primarily about managing people at all. The title, Manager, is about managing a department or function. To that end, staff members in the department are really a necessary evil to serve that purpose.

So, Why do you want to be a manager? The best reply to this question is this: "Because I want more responsibilities and I need a team to help me achieve company goals." It is not because you like people or want to lead people. The reality is that the higher positions within a company have a broad scope of responsibilities and goals that an individual cannot achieve alone. In fact, if you talk with experienced people managers and ask them if they enjoy the people management aspect of their job, most will tell you they tolerate it at best, and hate it at worst.-Notice that the rank and pay that comes with it naturally happens.

What's the catch?

Simply put, there's more work involved and the job is more difficult. There are no free lunches. The rank and higher pay is compensation for something and that something is 1) deliver the higher responsibilities and more challenging goals through a team of people and 2) you get to manage those people. People are difficult to manage. Many employees are incompetent or lazy or negative or criminal or mistake-prone, or all of the above. Even if only one employee is difficult, that's enough to create heartburn for you. And the paperwork and administration that goes along with managing people is tiresome, to say the least. Here is a list of just some of the paperwork and time commitments you can look forward to as a manager:

- goal setting for every direct staff member
- annual performance reviews for every direct staff member
- staff meetings
- one-on-one meetings
- meetings to reprimand staff members
- developing budgets
- termination processes and documentation
- personnel improvement plan (fancy term for a correction process for a poor performing employee)
- succession plan

- organization plan

- affirmative action plan

- interviews

- developing and documenting job descriptions

- salary reviews and recommendations

- and more

Being a manager can be such a hassle, I've known many mangers who went back to being an individual contributor (fancy term for non-people manager). Of course, some people are so fed up with being a manager, they will sacrifice the higher pay and accept a lower salary. So, be careful what you ask for. You want to mooove ahead. If you want the higher rank and commensurate compensation, then you will have to manage people. It doesn't mater how much you may enjoy people management, you'll have to be fairly savvy at it if you're going to be a successful manager. Remember, you can't do it alone.

Frustration of Unpredictability

For some people, they gave up on the desire and effort to become a manager. It can be frustrating. There is no defined time frame to becoming one. There are no paths or process. There are clearly no guarantees, despite how hard you work towards it.

How do job promotions *really* work? What role does your manager play? What is your next job? What is your career path and is it restricted to your current company, etc?

These are all questions people in the herd ask everyday, and have done since the advent of organization and rank.

The short answer is, there is no magic pill and there are no guarantees.

The long answer to getting promotions or getting hired as a manager involves a bit of luck, hard work, some natural and acquired hard and soft skills, networking, persistence, and bits of insights. This book will help with the insight part. The rest, unfortunately, is up to you.

We can check off the box for hard work, hard and soft skills, networking, and persistence. If you want to get ahead of the herd, you already know you need to do these things. They've been discussed in previous chapters. You can control these elements. Doing all these earns you a ticket into "the batter's box", so that you are given a chance to swing at the "ball"...the ball of opportunities (using a popular sports phrase you'll hear in the corporate hallways).

How often will you get into the batter's box and then how often will you hit a single vs. a home run or hit the ball at all?...that's the part that you can't really control precisely. There's this thing called "luck".

Luck is the least controllable element. It is a true variable that is unpredictable. I call it luck, but as the popular saying by Ernest Hemingway goes, "you make your own luck". The definition of "luck" is "The chance happening of fortunate or adverse events. ". Take "persistence". Persistence is not working hard. Persistence is constantly looking and inquiring about opportunities that resulted from a fortunate or adverse event (which may have been an unfortunate event for someone else, such as the person who lost the position you are trying to fill). It's asking your Manager, as described in earlier chapters. It's staying in touch with the job market and networks. It's always staying on top of activities that help to create luck, because luck consists, first and foremost, of timing. In the corporate world, those events are job opportunities that most often includes:

- Attrition, such as a previous person in a position who's been removed for various reasons

- New positions created due to company growth

- New positions created due to reorganization

- New positions created due to a specific company need (i.e. special project, company-wide initiative, a project to deal with a problem)

You cannot predict these scenarios; therefore you have to keep your eyes and ears open. We discussed in earlier sections about making internal and external networks and keeping in touch with them so you have insight into possible changes (and openings).

There's more to the "science" of why some people are luckier than others. J. D. Roth discussed this very well in his blog article – http://www.getrichslowly.org/blog/2009/01/29/how-to-make-your-own-luck/. J. D. Roth summarizes a recent *Newsweek* article by Ben Sherwood, January 24, 2009. According to J. D. Roth, Professor Wiseman in the article suggests four reasons that luck favors certain people:

1. **Lucky people frequently happen upon chance opportunities.** But this is more than just being in the right place at the right time. "Lucky" people also have to be *aware* or the opportunity, and have the courage to seize it. You know what they say: "Carpe Diem".

2. **Lucky people listen to their hunches.** In other words, they listen to their gut instinct. This reminds me of Malcolm Gladwell's *Blink*, which argues that often our first instincts are correct.

3. **Lucky people persevere in the face of failure.** You've all seen that Nike commercial from Michael Jordan, right? "I've missed more than 9000 shots in my career. I've lost almost 300 games. 26 times, I've been trusted to take the game winning shot and missed. I've failed over and over and over again in my life. And that is why I succeed."

4. **Lucky people have the ability to turn bad luck into good fortune.** The past couple of weeks have been pretty $#!++^ for me. They've sucked. It would be easy to surrender and just give up. Instead, I've tried to find the positive, and to build something constructive out of my experience. Instead of focusing on the loss of a close friend, I think, "What can I take from this?" As I wrote and delivered my eulogy, for example, I tried to learn more about speaking in public. (My second eulogy at tonight's memorial service should be even better.)

I encourage you to read the entire *Newsweek* article. It's well worth your time. And it may prove to be the luckiest thing you do all day!

It's lonely at the top

This statement doesn't hit you until, one day, you're a Director or VP and it's lunchtime and you realize that there are very few people who want to go out to lunch with you. That's when you think back to how different (carefree and fun) it was in the early days, when you were an individual contributor. Groups of people at that level would go out and enjoy a social activity. Everyone can talk and think freely while enjoying lunch. At each level of Management, the number and level of "fun" decreases until one day, you're experiencing a statement you may have heard early on but discounted – it really IS lonely at the top.

Not that you will have any lack of physical or social interaction with people or that you won't have lunch with people. The experience is much different. The people you interact with are different. There's less social freedom. You have to be more reserved. You have to be careful, even calculating as to what you can say. If it's with customers, you have to play a role. If it's with management peers, you have to be politically on-guard. If it's with upper executives, you have to put on a show. And if it's with your staff or lower level employees, you have to be a leader and be extremely careful with your words and statements. It's work. You're always on guard. It is not a nice social event. This is why they call it "work", not "social hour".

Another form of loneliness is being singled out. There are fewer Managers at each level of the pyramid, therefore these people standout….in many ways. The rock star aspect of recognition and being admired as a leader can be gratifying. Don't let it get to your head. Just like rock stars and celebrities, they live in a fishbowl with everyone watching their every move. Everything they do is magnified and amplified. It's great when they do good things, but when they do something controversial and unpopular, that's not so appealing. And there is constant gossip and criticism behind your back. Ironically, with all the people around them, celebrities are lonely. It's a paradox even in the corporate world. Employees are intimidated or don't know how to get close. Any interaction is very guarded both ways. It's plain awkward at best.

Is it all bad? No, but you need to be aware and act accordingly. There's a lot at risk, ranging from harassment to career limitation to reducing your leadership aura.

Still want to be a Manager?

Yes, of course you should! You're young. It's a learning experience. And you have nothing to lose. Best case, you are good at it and you're on your way to getting ahead of the herd. Worst case, you fail or you find you plain hate it. No problem. It's an experience and learning which nobody can take away from you, just like your college degree. You can always go back to being a non-manager.

Are you worried about failing? Failure is part of the learning and growth process. I know, it's an overused cliché about "learning from failure." In most companies, a person's failure does not linger or hurt the person's career long term. It's not that you failed. The important points are 1) you don't keep failing for the same reasons and 2) you recover well. Learn from your mistakes and your past experiences. Recovering well involves the attitude you move forward with, applying what you learned from the failure, and being persistent in pursuit of whatever you are working towards

The next chapter will discuss how to get into a position, to be promoted or hired into a manager position. We'll assume you will achieve a manager level, but that just puts you on the road to mooove ahead of the herd. You still have to prove you belong and can mooove ahead, so we will follow with chapters on how to be a successful manager.

Key Actions Checklist

☐ Be sure you want to be a manager for the right reasons. Talk to people who are or have been managers to get further insight. Then be open minded about whether you really are prepared and truly desire this path.

☐ Look up the blog by J. D. Roth – http://www.getrichslowly.org/blog/2009/01/29/how-to-make-your-own-luck/ where J. D. Roth summarizes a *Newsweek* article by Ben Sherwood, January 24, 2009.

Chapter 10 – Getting on the trail to mooove up the herd (in other words, how to become a manager.)

"Too often it's not the most creative guys or the smartest. Instead, it's the ones who are best at playing politics and soft-soaping their bosses. Boards don't like tough, abrasive guys." ~ Carl Icahn

I guess I didn't scare you off from the desire to becoming a manager. Still want to mooove ahead of the herd? Alright then, this chapter is about HOW to put yourself in a position to become one.

Predictable Paths

The paths that lead most people to a management position are predictable.

Fundamentally, there are three likely paths:

1. You become a leader (aka. Manager) of your function.

2. You switch functions, climb a new ladder, and become a leader of that function.

3. You switch functions several times and, hopefully, the stars will line up, given unique circumstances in previous employment situations, and this one will stick.

There are always exceptions, but they're not predictable. Someone with no experience gets hired as a manager or a Vice President decides to take a chance on a low level employee and promotes that person to a position several levels above. These things can happen. The odds are ridiculously low, but it can happen. It's not predictable, but it can happen.

Functional Skills

What you control, especially in your early career stage, is the advancement of your job function skills – a specialization. You'll figure out fairly soon whether you're good at that specialization, or not. For example, in the technical writing department the writing skills, output quality, and speed of an individual will likely set that individual apart from his/her department peers. Otherwise, the individual must look for another company or another function that he/she can specialize and excel at. It may be necessary to change companies to improve the skills you need or find higher levels (and pay) of the same function.

What you need to do is assess quickly what path you need to take. What I found difficult at this early stage for an individual is his/her awareness of where they are in their current path and whether that path is a dead-end. There are no clear signs. It's a little like poker – you have to know when to hold them and when to fold them. This is where talking with people, such as peers and mentors, can help give you some perspective and help you see the forest from the trees.

Get as much data as you can with respect to your performance. Ask your Manager where you stand and what skills you are missing to be considered for advancement. Sounds easy, but I know it's not when you're in the day-to-day work environment. I've been there and I know every situation appears unique, especially when you cannot see the trees for the forest. I also learned that you wouldn't necessarily think about your path until it's too late or some event occurs at work that triggers you to assess your situation. I encourage you to regularly find ways to get more data and find ways to step back to look at the forest. Again, I cannot stress enough the importance of consulting with your mentors, especially someone outside the company you work at. They are not caught up in the day-to-day duties and pressures of your job (and your life.) They can give you valuable outside perspective. They can also ask insightful and probing questions you did not consider. They can objectively assess your company and its marketplace. They can offer you what we now know as career coaching.

Be the best employee and be the best at your job

This seems obvious, but if it is so obvious and simple, why are so many individual contributors aching to be promoted but are not? One reason is that many employees are not as good as they can be (or they don't work hard enough or they work on the wrong things.).

As a manager, I observed that an employee's perception of himself or herself is often far different from the perception of others (not just their direct manager, but others in the organization as well.)

I've been involved in several companies that used the "360-degree" method for annual performance reviews. This review approach enlists feedback about an employee from their peers, their supervisor, fellow employees that interact daily with the employee, and, in some cases, people outside the company, such as suppliers, vendors, and customers. Thus the term "360-degree" job performance – the feedback is from all around. In my experience, the gap between the employee's perception of their performance versus what others around them thought or their overall job performance was very wide.

If you are the best employee and you are the best at your job, there is a good chance that you will be promoted. I've seen this happen. It is not a guarantee, but you will definitely put yourself in a good position if you stand out among the herd. Conversely, if you are a poor employee (e.g. are very negative, tardy, not a team player, etc.) and/or you are one of the worst at your job function, I can almost *guarantee* that you won't get promoted. Being a poor employee is *not* a good way to stand out.

Let your Manager know of your career plans

Here's another recommendation that will make you ask: "Really?" Isn't it obvious?" If so, you're either smarter or braver than the average cow, because I rarely had employees do it with me. Fellow managers tell me they have rarely had employees freely do it with them either. Even when asked, most employees can't effectively tell their Manager what their career plans are in a way that allows the Manager to help them.

When I first started out in corporate life, one of my managers, a wise Asian gentleman, told me, "You need to tell your Manager what you want. It's not like in the movies: they don't come chasing you to promote you just because you are good at your job. This is especially true for Asians because Asians traditionally are quiet and do not want to create a fuss." What I have learned since then is that Asians' are not the only employees who are "quiet" and reserved about sharing their career desires. But-I got my manager's point: You need to express your career plans with your manager, even if you are not asked.

So how and when do you bring up your career plans with your Manager? "When" is any time you have-his/her undivided attention, such as during your performance review. I recommend that you request a performance appraisal meeting after you have been at a job for four to six months. Some people might wait to be approached at a meeting of this nature, given that performance appraisals are often dreaded. However, if you are a good employee, you have nothing to be worried about, and the meeting should be a learning experience (not to mention yet another chance to stand out from the rest of the herd). You want to establish early on with your Manager where you are headed and that you need help from him/her. At the annual performance review, you have another formal opportunity to talk about your plans. If your Manager tells you that there are no opportunities for you, but that it has nothing to do with you or your skills, then your days at this company are numbered. Accept the reality that there's no future there. You should plan on leaving, but-stay long enough to learn all you can, and log a reasonable time at this company on your resume (one to two years minimum).

Conversely, it is likely that your Manager will be receptive to your plans, and she/he may know exactly how to help you. If not, you can help him or her to help you. To do this, find out what types of opportunities exist in your department, your division, and your company. Ask your Manager to help you identify areas where you need to improve or expand your skills in order to realistically qualify for open positions. Then, in subsequent meetings, you can share what you've done to improve or grow, and get feedback from your Manager on what they think of your progress. When you use this approach, your Manager will consciously and sub-consciously identify job openings for which you are suited, as he/she goes about daily interactions with peer managers.

Beware that a Manager's greatest fear is losing a good staff member

Understand that one thing that can impede your getting promoted is that your manager is going to have fears about losing you as a staff member. You can help ease this by helping your manager develop others in your department, improve the department processes and procedures so that the department functions better and is not dependent upon any one employee, and assist in identifying a replacement for you in the event that you leave for another position. This last point could involve collecting resumes of qualified candidates, helping with interviews, training new employees (even *after* you start your new positions), and so on.

The Paradox

Companies have a dilemma when they consider promoting the best employee in a department. This dilemma is two fold. For one, the best employee in a function does not necessarily have the skills to be a successful, competent manager. Secondly, by promoting a very good employee, the company is essentially losing a strong player in the function that is being vacated by the promoted employee. The conventional wisdom to justify this type of promotion is to establish the expectation that the employee-turned-Manager will become a mentor/coach and will be able to develop other employees into filling his shoes.

Unfortunately, studies have shown (and I've seen for myself), that conventional wisdom and meaningful intentions do not work as predicted in the corporate world for exactly the reason given above: *A Manager requires a skill set that is very different than the skill set required to be a successful individual contributor.*

Most individual contributor positions are technically and functionally oriented while a Manager requires many different, even diametrically opposite skills. The following table details some of the differences between the requirements for an individual contributor and a manager. It is important to recognize these differences, and to keep the company's potential paradox in mind when you are lobbying for a position in management.

Individual Contributor	Manager
Task-oriented, process driven, governed by established practices; tactical	Defines tactics to achieve goals; strategic
Very specific goals (e.g., number of calls completed, project completion on schedule, number of journal entries, etc.)	Goals are broader in nature (e.g., increase productivity by 5%; increase sales by 20%; reduce cycle time; create new product line, etc.)
Responsible for self, not others	Responsible for others; mentor, train, coach, reprimand, hire, fire
Few or no leadership attributes are measured	Leadership attributes required to achieve goals and to operate effectively within the organization
Limited interaction with other functions and levels	Interaction and reliance on broad range of corporate functions and levels
Limited empowerment for decision-making and use of resources	Define and direct allocated resources

Chicken or Egg?

How do you learn and demonstrate manager skills when you are not a Manager? That's one of the tricks to this whole game. What you should not do is take a negative bent on this challenge. Remember what one of my previous VP told me, "You need to work 8:00am to 5:00pm at your current job, and 5:00pm to 8:00am for your next job." Simply put, he was saying you couldn't come to work and put only your normal time in and expect to get ahead. You have to invest in developing new skills and behaviors in order to prove yourself. This investment will likely take some time.

In the past, I regularly had staff members tell me that they were not going to do work outside their "normal" paid hours without additional compensation. Did they miss the boat or what?! That is such a transactional, shortsighted approach. Even great athletes like Michael Jordan, Roger Federer, and Tiger Woods put in tremendous amounts of unpaid time and work early on so that they could get ahead. And they continue to work to maintain and improve their skills behind the scenes. You don't hear them complaining about not getting immediate compensation for all the work.

Think about ways to learn or exercise aspects of the categories below. Get ideas from mentors and even your manager.

Manager's Skills	Ways to demonstrate/learn
Must define tactics to achieve goals; practice strategic thinking	Ask to participate on new project teams and strategy teams, possibly to represent your manager's department. These teams generally start out with a problem or high-level goal and then the team must develop tactics to solve the problem or attain the goal. Participating in a strategy team provides great experience, while allowing you to contribute and hopefully show others and your Manager that you have strategic vision.
Broader goals (e.g., increase productivity by 5%; increase sales by 20%; reduce cycle time, create new product line, etc.)	Pay attention to the goals set for your company/division and subsequent goals derived for departments within the company/division. Understand what the goals mean, why they are what they are, and how they align with other established company goals all the way up to the President's goals. Again, don't hesitate to ask a mentor within the company or your Manager if you need help understanding the goals. Suggest to your manager what you can do to support his/her goals.
Responsible for others; mentor, train, coach,	If you cannot formally be promoted, ask your Manager if there is an opportunity to "intern" in some capacity that will allow you to practice and

reprimand, hire, fire	hone your people management and leadership skills. Ask to lead a team (such as a project team), take on the role of "guide" for new hires, participate in the hiring process, cover for a supervisor/manager while they are on vacation, etc. Brainstorm to get more ideas.
Leadership attributes required to achieve goals and operate effectively within the organization	Leadership is a difficult skill to quantify because leadership consists of a number of characteristics. If you ask most people for their opinion regarding an employee's leadership abilities or potential, they will usually offer a "feeling" rather than a quantitative list. That feeling is developed through experience watching someone in action. The actions can be what a person accomplishes or a person's traits, including an assessment of the person being reliable, confident, and positive; and having the ability to take initiative, make timely decisions, communicate well orally and in writing; and being able to get others to participate in a goal and produce good work. If you aspire to a leadership role, you need to demonstrate these traits at every opportunity. A fellow employee had a great quote: "If you acted the position, the authorities would have given it to you." That's similar to, "If you act like a leader, you will be treated like one."
Interaction and reliance on broad range of corporate functions and levels	You need to learn about what other departments do; their goals, their challenges, what they rely on, their processes, and so on. You can't learn this from a book or class. Learn it firsthand from people in those departments. Focus on the functions/departments that interact most with your department/function.
Define and direct allocated resources	Start with learning to read and understand a financial statement and budget. If your company is public, there are financial statements in the annual report and quarterly results in 10-Ks the company is required to report to the investor community. If your company is private, you will have to hunt it down through a finance contact or your Manager. Ask your Manager to share your department's budget and actuals-to-date. Learn how budgets are developed. It's really not a mystery if you have

	participated in a budget creation session, but most of you won't until you are department managers or project managers. Invest the time to learn it now because knowing what your Manager is operating under can help you in many situations. Ask him/her to show you the budget and walk you through it. Review Chapter 7 about gaining Corporate Finance knowledge.

Tony's Stories

I remember when I was attending San Jose City College in the mid-1970s and everyday I had to walk through the track field to get to my Electronics classes.   Each and every morning I saw this young man practicing when I walked to class and four hours later when I walked back to my car. Everyday this person would throw javelins, run sprints, toss discus, high jump, pole vault, and so on, over and over again. I remember thinking, "What is that guy working so hard for? Can he make a living in Track & Field? Maybe he should get a degree in Electronics (like me) so he has a chance to make a living?" A couple of years later, 1976 to be precise, I learned that person I had seen practicing was Bruce Jenner. Bruce Jenner won the Olympic Gold medal and set a world record in Decathlon at the 1976 Summer Olympics. Jenner was also named the Associated Press Male Athlete of the Year. While Jenner was practicing at San Jose City College prior to the 1976 Olympics, he and his wife lived in a small apartment. He worked in the afternoon and on weekends at some low-paying job. His then wife had a full-time job and was the main wage earner. They lived from small paycheck to small paycheck. If Jenner subscribed to the thought, "I'm not going to practice unless I get paid for my practice time," do you think he would have accomplished his feats? After his gold medal performance, Jenner gained significant fortune and fame (and I'm LOL to this day that I ever thought that Jenner should have majored in Electronics).

It's a number's game. Make sure there are Manager slots open

There are only so many management jobs. You can't control it but you can recognize it and take action, such as leave for another organization.

Do the organizational math – on the average, there are eight employees to every supervisor/manager. The ratio is probably even worse, but I'm using the recommended ideal effective management ratio expressed by the management gurus and in various studies.

During a recession (as this book is being written, we are currently in the worst one since the crash of 1929), many companies cut management positions, causing the employee-to-manager ratio to go even higher. Even in good economic times, certain functions, such as manufacturing and call centers, have ratios as high as 30-to-1. The sad reality is that organizational structures are pyramids, with fewer leadership jobs as you near the top of the pyramid. This means that employees must compete with their peers for the few available management positions. So even if an employee is good, he or she is not good enough if others are better. The point is that when there are so few management positions available, only the best employees stand a chance at getting promoted into them. If the organizational math at your company tells you that there is no room for you (or anyone) to be promoted, you may want to move to another company where there is room. Why be a backup quarterback sitting on the bench when you could be a starting quarterback for some other team whose short on good quarterbacks?

Be available

Be available so your management has more options is related to the concept of "Managing Up," discussed earlier in Chapter 8. Being available simply means that you need to be a flexible and versatile resource for your manager.

Managers consistently have tasks and situations where they need someone to help. For example, your department is going to outsource some tasks to a business center in India. This project demands that a number of tasks be completed in order for the outsource transition to be successful. Key tasks include: developing and documenting processes and procedures, training the Indian team, and managing the project. The challenge for your Manager is to identify very knowledgeable employees with subsets of these skills to accomplish these tasks. The more skills you demonstrate, the more you become available to your Manager as a resource for one of more tasks on this very important project. Be the go-to person that your Manager can rely upon and knows will be available should they need you for an important task.

Physically speaking, you have to be visible. Don't hide in your cubicle. Change is constant and inevitable in corporations, especially reorganizations. It happens in every corporation, constantly. You can't control structural change, but you can benefit from it by being more valuable within the organization. Being a versatile resource, along with all the virtues I've previously advocated about being a great employee in general, may help you gain a better position during a corporate change, such as a reorganization or a merge with another company.

Volunteer for the tough assignments

If you want to get ahead of the herd, and eventually get promoted, you need to ask for the tough assignments. This is the acid test for determining how afraid you are of failure. Your willingness to confidently take on the tough assignments is generally only limited by how concerned you are with failing. All that stuff you read or hear about successful people and how they succeeded only because they failed somewhere along the way, there's a lot of truth to it.

Up to this point in the book, hopefully I've pounded that point home so much that you are dreaming about investing in yourself, learning skills, learning from others, and learn all you can even if the dots don't seem to connect yet. The reality is that most people will never have all the skills and experiences to guarantee success at any tough assignment. That's why the assignments are tough! And that's why you want tough (and perhaps more importantly, visible) assignments. Worst case, you fail but you learned from the experience. And if you lead the assignment correctly, you've involved enough people so you increase your chance of success. Not to mention that if you still fail, you won't fail alone. *Don't fail alone. Never fail alone.* Unless you are completely incompetent, most people and organizations forget and forgive failure. With tough assignments, prepare for the frustration and difficulty to make progress. That's part of the learning. It's invaluable even if you cannot see the value during the trial. This is what all those successful people meant about succeeding AFTER failures. Overcoming the failure itself is a toughening experience in and of itself. Because history tends to repeat itself, you will learn to avoid and/or overcome mistakes in the future because you've been there, done that. If you don't try, you're playing it safe, you also did not separate yourself from the herd. A common business saying based on the game of baseball sums it up perfectly – when you get a chance in the batter's box, swing at the ball. If you don't swing the bat, you will never hit the ball.

Last Cow Standing

If you can't beat your competition to a manager position, you might be able to outlast them to one.

When a company is growing dramatically, people are promoted simply because they're available. The opposite happens, too. When a company goes through difficult times, employees leave or they are let go. There are many examples of difficult times, not all are a result of economic conditions. Other things that create difficulties for companies include company relocation, acquiring another company, being acquired by another company, and internal reorganizations. During difficult times, poor performers are often let go and sometimes, even good performers including managers leave the company voluntarily. The company cannot control or prevent the good performers from leaving. These situations open up opportunities for the remaining "best" performers. I have seen a fair number of incidences whereby a person was promoted simply because he/she was the best of the people left in the department.

When the company you work for is going through a difficult time, the challenge for you is to determine the best path for your career. If you are one of the last cows standing, staying with the company may mean that there is a possibility of getting promoted; this would give you valuable experience and add a notch to your resume. However, staying may require you to tolerate all the negative aspects of the situation. Depending on the situation, this could mean having to do the jobs of three people, working for a terrible boss, relocating, working in an environment with poor morale, and so on. You may choose to leave for greener pastures. If you choose to stay, I would certainly recommend that you hedge your bets by keeping an active job hunt going so that you have choices.

You may be wondering, "Aren't there normal conditions for promotional opportunities?" The answer is, "not really." Opportunities surface because there is change. As the saying goes, "Generals are made in wartime." In the military, promotions are less frequent during times of peace than times of war. During wartime, the troop count increases, so there is a need for more commanders (managers.) Those who are promoted are soldiers who have proven themselves in actual combat.

In business, change is constant. Like a soldier at battle, you must prove yourself through successfully accomplishing your goals, projects, and assignments. All the talk, classes, degrees, and planning do not prove you are promotional material unless you show that you can implement. You want the challenge. You want the problems to solve. You want the tough projects and assignments. You want the business "war" to fight and to prove yourself.

Get superiors to be comfortable with you and your style

"Cows of a spot, pack together." (I know, I know. The saying goes, "Birds of a feather flock together", but this is a book using cow analogies!) This holds true in the corporate world (and the world, period), whether you like it or not. At the risk of being labeled a racist, which I am not, the reality even in the 21st century is that people are still people and people tend to surround themselves with people that they like and are comfortable with. I label myself as a *realist*. My observation (and backed by surveys of the makeup of Corporate America's C-level people) is that corporate leaders are still predominately Caucasian men. Debate all you want about whether this is good or bad, but it is what it is today. I'm not here to debate truisms. This book is not about becoming an activist. This book is to give you insight into the very real landscape and obstacles in corporate life so that you can navigate them better and faster. In the corporate world, for the sake of your career, it is a safer bet to assume the above as a truism, then to bet on idealism and have to adjust from there.

That being said, the point is that you need to do, act, and conform in ways that will make your immediate Manager as comfortable with you as possible. You also need to extend this concept to your Manager's Manager because he/she has a say in promotions. Therefore, if your corporate leader is Mickey Mouse, you need to understand what makes Mickey Mouse comfortable and then conform. How do you do this? Unfortunately there is no hard and fast way or a 10-step process. This is an art. There is a feel to it, and it can be very situational.

It is impossible to anticipate all potential situations, but here are some general guidelines:

Do your homework on the people you report to

What do they like? What do they do outside of work? What is their background? What college did they graduate from? And so on. It's okay to ask them when you have a chance to get in some small talk. Note what their interpersonal tendencies are in group meetings, one-on-one meetings, and in social situations. If you were hired by your Manager, you already have great insight because of what you observed and what you asked of him/her during the interview.

Complement the style of the person you are interacting with

Use the *Myers-Briggs* personality matrix mentioned in Chapter 2. It provides a good foundation to understand your personality and how to work with other personality types.

Withhold sharing radical aspects of your personality and life.

This means that in your corporate life, be conservative and stay away from potentially volatile topics. Stay away from declaring your religious, political, sexual beliefs, and affiliations. Also, I wouldn't recommend you share the tattoo you have on your back, as that's probably not a way to stand out from the herd in a positive way ;-).

Become interested in your superior's interest

For example, if your Manager graduated from Ohio State, learn something about that university and engage him/her in conversation when you can. Buckeye alumni are usually rabid about their football. Many of my staff members over the years did not understand why sports are often so important to senior leaders (most of whom were men). I finally asked the employees why it was important to them to waste brainpower on this question. Their reply revealed more than curiosity. They were actually resentful. They resented that the senior leaders were mostly men. They were resentful how low on the totem pole they were. Since they connected sports with the senior leaders, sports became a symbol of their resentment, and, therefore, they hated sports. I asked these staff members why they were not open to learning about and appreciating sports to get better insight into the leadership team? They thought I was smoking something. I explained to them that the first step in becoming a senior leader (at least in most of the existing corporations in this world) is to conform and adapt. I further explained how sports fit into the men's world, and the parallels between business and sports. Finally, I related that if the company we worked at had a senior leadership team that was predominantly female, I would learn to appreciate the things those leaders found interesting.

Be open to learning many different topics. Remember some of my early advice about constant learning, variety, and how dots eventually connect? If you have been practicing this advice, you will find that it is likely to pay off when you pursue advancement into management.

Key Actions Checklist

☐ Commit yourself to be functionally the best in your department/company.

☐ Develop more skills; extend your experience and skills.

☐ Regularly meet with your manager to get feedback about your performance, ask for career advice, and ask for opportunities to develop more skills especially those that will transfer into managerial skills listed in the table.

☐ Identify mentors and skip-level sessions.

☐ Assess promotional opportunities at your present company– Can you be the best? Is your specialization suited for you? Are there enough managerial slots openings?

☐ Practice the non-tangible behaviors that can help you get ahead of the corporate herd.

Chapter 11 – Preparing for People Management

"A good manager is best when people barely know that he exists. Not so good when people obey and acclaim him. Worse when they despise him."
~ Lao Tzu

(Chinese Taoist Philosopher, founder of Taoism, 600 BC-531 BC)

Originally I was planning to combine this chapter with the previous chapter. After all, people management is the obvious central activity of managing down.

I did not do it because 1) practically speaking the chapter would have been too long and 2) I would have lost your attention on this key discussion.

Managing people is the core, vital practice for Managers. I stress "practice". Just like lawyers practice law, managers practice managing people because few people naturally are experts on day one. Managing people is more art than science, intangible than tangible, situation-based than cookie cutter-based, experience-driven than academic-driven.

As was mentioned earlier, the greatest challenge as a manager is managing your herd effectively. The technical part of your responsibility and departmental function is relatively easy. You've been focused most of your life on the technical aspects. All your schooling has been to learn facts, information, theories, lab work, and so forth. Where have you learned about people? Formally it might have been in one or two classes, such as Organizational Behavior, Sociology, or perhaps Psychology. Informally you may have been exposed to organizations and activities such as Boy's Scout, Student Government, Fraternities, and other clubs.

You may not have realized it, but you experienced all the good and bad of people in organized activities. Hopefully you experienced it both as a member in the group as well as a leader of the group. Managing people is difficult. People are unpredictable, conniving, calculating, complex, in addition to being a myriad of other things.

If managing people are such an important part of being a manager, why isn't there more training? The answer is irrelevant at this point. The better question at this point is, how do you prepare to be good at it sooner?

Let me present my accelerated version of People Management 101. It's a completely different approach than the traditional, old school method.

Tony's Stories

For me, I thought if I do my best at my job and train to be a manager, it'd happen. It didn't quite work out that way. Early in my career when I was at Apple Computer, I did my job pretty well and received high praise and excellent reviews from my Manager. My Manager, in fact, recommended me for the Apple Manager Survival Course. This was a big deal. The course was a weeklong retreat at the Claremont Hotel in the Oakland Hills. Not a cheap date! Apple was a very progressive, young company with very young employees. The average age of employees in 1987 was only 29 years old. And the company's growth was meteoric. They were adding 50 employees a week at their corporate campus in Cupertino, California, and had to hold two employee orientations per week to accommodate. The company had enough realization and foresight to invested heavily in training to help their young employees to mature and develop leadership skills quickly, particularly people management skills. The growth was so tremendous that it was common for individual contributors (who were not hired with previous people management experience), such as secretaries, accounting clerks, and Product Managers, to be promoted within a year to manage some new department or to take over the reins of their current department because their Manager was promoted or moved to lead another department.

The Manager Survival Course was very good but it did not get me a Manager's job. I did not get promoted to be a Manager for four years. When I was finally promoted into a Manager position, I had forgotten most of what the course taught and I was not smart enough to review the notes and workbook from the course. Life, personal and business, has a way of moving very fast and consuming all of your time. And, to be quite honest, half of what I learned in that Survival Course did not stick. Much of the content was not relevant because I was not a practicing Manager, so it was difficult for me to relate. It's like being taught how to raise a child when you are single with no children. I believe it would have been more helpful to take a shorter, introduction course before becoming a Manager. Then take a detailed class, like the Survival Course, after you've been a Manager for at least 6 months.

People Management 101 (Tony's version)

I really was very lucky early in my career. I had all sorts of corporate training. I had extensive sales training at NCR; and I was given books and countless skills classes at Apple and HP. I was provided a mentorship program at Apple and given a gazillion books, classes, seminars, and articles about how to manage people. Some of these charge a hefty amount. If you're fortunate enough, your company will pay for them. All my previous employers did. I was very lucky to have access to so many resources.

Despite all the formal training, managing people was a foreign activity. In retrospect, managing people really is an art and all the academics only helped to a limited degree.

There is science behind it, but you still have to recognize the situation and know which tool to use. I have learned there is no one formula or one method to help people learn the intricacy of this topic. I've also learned that all the reading and classes are fine, however, you still need real life experience. By all means, go to the classes and read all the books. As I've stated, it helped me to some degree. The way I learn, I needed other examples and modes of learning. Everybody learns differently; some are visual learners, some need written instructions, some need hands-on, and so forth. Personally, I learn best by watching examples and having something I am familiar with to compare them to. I'm going to share with you two people management models that helped me break through the mechanics and academics of people management and leadership to where it felt more natural.

1. Manage people like you raise children or dogs.

Alright, suspend the criticism about comparing adult employees with kids, at least until you finish hearing me out conceptually. When I was first given this golden concept, I did not have children and I was not much of a dog person. Therefore, this golden concept made no sense to me until a couple of years later after the birth of my daughter. About the same time, my wife (a natural dog whisperer) started a pet-sitting business and I began learning about dogs from her. The idea made perfect sense and I learned to apply it effectively with employees. I found nearly all of the principles used to raise kids and dogs carried over perfectly to managing people.

Praise when good behavior occurs. It's true with people (kids and adults) and with dogs – praise good behavior (as close to the moment it occurs) and they will be motivated to repeat the behavior. At a raw level, this is a predictable action-reaction. Of course people are different than dogs from an intelligence perspective, in that people have a broader understanding of "good behavior". Dogs will repeat the identical behavior they were rewarded for. People will repeat a general definition of the behavior. In other words, if a person is praised for being punctual on turning in a report, he/she understands the reward was for being punctual in general, not solely for the report. A dog on the other hand would associate the praise exactly to the report and not with attendance, project completion, or other work aspects.

Correct poor behavior as close to when it occurs as possible to make the association. One other difference between dogs and people is the time association. Dogs have no sense of time and recall, therefore any praise or correction must be done right at the point it occurs. Ever notice that a dog will wait all day seemingly without any realization of how long they've been waiting? With people, you can discuss the incident many days after the fact and they will still associate it. Given enough time though, people will likely forget the situation or details and you will lose effectiveness. Once the time association is established, you can praise or reprimand behavior.

Exception Warning: It is not a good idea to correct bad behavior (and sometimes applies to good behavior) immediately if it's going to be a public situation. An effective Manager would realize that reprimanding an employee in public is not in the best interests of anyone involved. Reprimanding an employee in public may be effective in terms of setting an example, however you can still get this effect while minimizing potential drawbacks by delaying the commendation. Some employees are embarrassed by public recognition. Giving recognition to an employee is equally, if not more, effective when done privately. And if a public recognition opportunity is available, the Manager can ask the employee if he/she would participate. When it comes to reprimanding an employee, the modern approach (based on political correctness, legal exposure, and organizational behavior research) is to discuss poor performance in private, and possibly with a Human Resource representative in the meeting with you.

Show care and respect as often as possible. Treating kids and dogs with disrespect is a form of abuse. The result is, generally, kids and dogs that exhibit many forms of psychological damage. The same goes for treating employees with disrespect. Unlike dogs or kids, employees are more prone to leave. Showing employees care and respect is a relatively recent practice in the USA corporate world. It was less than 40 years ago that American Managers did NOT show care or respect for employees. Employees were simply tools to get a job done. Managing with a stick, not with sugar, was the norm. Watch the recent TV series, Mad Men, for an excellent rendition of the work environment between 1959-1960's – and this was a white-collar work environment. We can only imagine how bad the blue-collar environment was. For that matter, most developing countries today seem to be where the USA was 40 years ago. As these countries' economies expand, they too are feeling the effects of turnover and dissatisfied employees.

Get their attention before giving instructions/orders. All the great dog whisperers on TV use a technique when giving instruction to a dog: they get the dog's attention, making eye contact, and only then do they give a command; same goes with kids. Yelling orders to the kids in the other room is not very effective. Kids (and dogs) are so easily distracted. Remember the scene in the movie, "Up", where the dogs are easily distracted at the sight (or thought) of a squirrel? You have to get their attention up-close. This technique applies when Managers want to make their communications as effective as possible. For example, when a Manager is having a one-on-one meeting with a staff member and the topic will be emotional, such as discussing inappropriate behavior or poor performance with the staff member, the Manager should make sure he/she has the staff member's attention and the staff member is ready for the discussion. Tell the staff member what the topic is and ask if this is a good time to talk about it. Look them in the eye and make sure they are acknowledging the situation. Another example would be when a Manager is giving instructions/directions on what he/she needs the staff member(s) to do. An email might suffice, but when it must be absolutely clear, the communication should absolutely be in person. Just as the saying goes about good presentation format – tell them what you need, give them the detail, and then tell them what you just told them. With a dog whose attention can be easily distracted (recall the movie, Up, and what happens to dogs when they see a squirrel?), make sure you get eye contact and acknowledgment that the staff member(s) hear and understand the communication/direction/instruction/etc (head nods, uh hum's, questions, etc.). You would be surprised how often staff members 1) didn't hear everything, 2) had selective hearing, and/or 3) nod or say yes to everything even when they don't agree or don't understand or are scared/embarrassed to admit they don't understand (the ole' Asian smile and nod routine).

Review performance more frequently early on after new instruction. When there is a new employee or new instruction/project assigned to an inexperienced employee, the Manager should manage more closely at the beginning and let go "of the rope" over time when the employee and/or project illustrates the ability to progress correctly to goal and within acceptable out-of-bounds criteria. This approach applies to both dogs and children. In the modern age of Management, the needle leans towards delegate and trust probably a bit too far and too fast. Perhaps the real issue is incorrectly mixing "trust" and "delegate" in the same sentence. They are mutually exclusive. Inexperienced Managers don't understand this. An adult would not let a 15 years old child drive solo the very first time behind the wheel of a car; similarly a Manager would not let a staff member go solo on their very first complex project.

Lead, manage and teach by example. "Do as I say, not as I do" is a saying that sarcastically pokes fun of people who do not lead by example. Staff members and employees develop loyalty, respect, and in some cases, skill sets by mimicking their superiors. Kids do the same with adults. Dogs, in some ways, take it even further; they sense what you really mean. Still, you have to really mean it, not just fake it. A perfect case in point, though not earth shattering in its consequence, still illustrates this concept well – starting time of meetings. Meetings are a way of life in the corporate world. What I've experienced is that the higher the level of Managers participating (and worst, leading) a meeting, the later the meeting starts relative to its advertised start time. Staff members continually experience this tardiness, and soon tardiness becomes part of the culture practiced at the lower levels. The executives talk about productivity and effectiveness, but they practice the opposite. When meetings don't start on time and people are scattering in randomly like popcorn popping, everyone's time is wasted. People that came on time are waiting for everyone else. Even if the meeting starts, the meeting often is not effective because key people are not at the meeting. Time is wasted when conversation is repeated for the latecomers or the latecomers ask previously asked questions because they were not there to hear what conversations have occurred. Overall, the team is out of synch. There are endless examples, but you get the main point.

Be consistent. This concept is easy to understand, but difficult to do. Staying the course is great on paper but in real life, situations can make being consistent difficult because you are tempted to take short cuts. You know giving your young child candy before dinner will reduce their appetite, not to mention promote cavities. Don't give in because of a weak moment. You're likely training your dog and child the wrong behavior. You're also teaching them that you do not have a standard. Your standard can be changed (with enough begging). This concept of being consistent can be risky when you consistently practice the wrong things. Being consistently inconsistent is not the goal. Using the meeting example, always attend and/or start a meeting on time. So when you think it's okay to be late because it's only "this one time" or "it's been a long time" or "this isn't a big deal" or "this won't hurt anything", think again what the cost is. The cost is your staff's perception of you and the culture you are trying to convey and lead. It's very difficult to create a positive brand, but easy to lose all that integrity with one "little" slip up. Stay consistent. And when you trip up, make sure you cover and recover well. Your staff will learn from that too.

Raise them to leave the nest (*don't raise them to be reliant upon you*). As a Manager, you should strive to grow your staff to eventually "leave the nest", which can mean getting promoted away from your department. It could be within your corporation or it could be in another corporation altogether. And the growth can take all different amounts of time for each staff member. The same goes for how you raise kids. You are raising them to go out into the world on their own and be as successful as they can be. For dogs, the parallel works in the case of rescue dogs. Rescue dogs are trained on many skills so they can be sent out to various assignments. Back to people management – the notion of a Manager helping to get their best staff members to leave seems counter-intuitive. A Manager wants to reach their goals and he/she needs a strong staff to do it. So why would the Manager want the hassle (and risk) of causing unnecessary turnover and jeopardize his/her ability to achieve his/her goals? The truth of the matter is, they don't. There is a loose "suggestion" in the corporate executive levels to develop from within, grow leadership, blah blah blah. The fact is, few if any corporations have a directive or any sort of review of this "philosophy." That's what it really is, a philosophy, with no teeth or incentive driving the implementation. I have a different approach and reasoning as to why a Manager should employ this approach: *you will achieve and likely exceed your goals because your staff will overachieve.* Two reasons, 1) they will be motivated by the prospect of advancement and the chance you're giving them and 2) they will do better work as they develop and round out their skills.

Alpha dog. Dogs are pack animals. That means they are social animals that like to belong to groups. Among any group, and depending on the group size, there is an Alpha dog. The Alpha dog is the leader whom the rest of the group members follow, look to please, and to receive adoration from. In the wild, most dogs want to be a pack member. They like to follow. Alpha dog status is an attitude and a skill that, for some reason, only a few dogs exhibit while the majority of dogs settle as followers. People behave in very similar ways, even in the workplace. In the workplace, the Manager is the Alpha Dog by position/authority, but not necessarily due to social status, skill, or respect terms. Therefore, to help make your job as a people manager easier, earning Alpha Dog status requires you to earn it by doing all the leadership traits well, the prominent ones being: 1. Honest, 2. Forward-Looking, 3. Competent, 4. Inspiring, and 5. Intelligent. You will be infinitely more effective getting the most from people who desire to follow up based upon respect (ala Alpha Dog) than by authority. Moreover, one way a Manager can be an effective leader is to win over the Alpha Dogs among the employee group. This is particularly useful if you have a large staff and if you have additional levels of staff reporting to you. The workplace has multiple Alpha Dogs. As mentioned, you are the Alpha Dog by authority and perhaps also by respect. At the employee level where the daily work is performed, there are employees that will assume an Alpha Dog role because of many factors, including tenure, social status, and knowledge/expertise. Knowing whom these Alpha Dogs are and how to get their support can help you get things done.

Spots (aka. personalities) don't change. The subject of couples trying to change each other is a hot topic. Millions of dollars are spent on research. There are numerous books on the subject. Talks shows discuss it all the time. People are fascinated because people want a solution to handling people. It doesn't matter what environment a person is in or what interaction a person has with others. **Golden rule: A person's behavior is what it is – you can't change it.** Great advice about people and their behavior has been available for hundreds, maybe thousands of decades. Yet, all the books and talk shows continue to thrive by communicating the same advice in different ways so that they are able to sell more. By the way, the advice applies to animals and kids too – spots can't be changed. People's (employee's) behavior don't change AND you can't change them; despite all the classes and training companies spend money on. Accept this truism and you will have less of a headache at work and less heartache at home.

At this point, I suspect the majority of you reading this recently graduated from college and likely do not have a child and you probably never thought about dogs other than they need feeding, loving, and their poop cleaned up. So you're thinking, "great, so I'm not going to be a good manager because the book says you need to have a child or a dog". Not at all. I've summarized the key aspects above so you know now, instead of years later. Additionally, your brain is adept enough to think through the advice and apply aspects of it effectively (you made it through college, didn't you?). One day, many of you will have your own kids and dogs and you will marvel at how correct the concepts below are. For me, it was an "ah-ha" moment when I figured it out because I did not have the benefit of this book and the foresight of the concepts.

2. Star Trek: Next Generation.

What??? A TV show and a sci-fi, at that? What does Star Trek have to do with managing people in the corporate world? As silly as this may seem, I'm serious. Yes, I admit I was (am) a geek, but just hear me out. If you've never watched the Star Trek: Next Generation and the Star Trek: Voyager series, go watch a few episodes. I'm sure there are other TV series that are models of good people management skills. These were mine.

The Manager role model in the Star Trek: Next Generation series was Captain Jean Luc Picard and in the Star Trek: Voyager series was Captain Katherine Janeway. Interestingly enough, both roles were designed along very similar leadership behaviors. For me, the Captain Jean Luc Picard character and the manner in which he managed and lead his crew was a big influence on me. I suspect that character influenced a generation of Managers during the show's run from 1987-1994.

Perhaps it was not an accident during that era for the show's writers to model what they thought leadership and management would be (should be) like in the 24th century. During the early 1980's, a progressive shift began in how Managers should manage—more humanistic, more respect, delegate, motivate, support, and mentor. High technology companies undoubtedly had a major influence, as did many groundbreaking management research studies and books. This new concept of managing people humanly and motivating people through reward to achieve maximum employee performance required a change in leadership and management style. Jean Luc Picard (and later continued with Katherine Janeway) illustrated the new leadership and management style to a worldwide audience.

Confidence. It didn't matter if Jean Luc and the crew of the USS Enterprise were in peril or not, Jean Luc was calm, cool, and positive. He never got too excited nor was he negative. He kept an even keel. He never stopped searching for a solution to a problem. He believed in himself and he believed in his crew. He never stopped learning. He had a curiosity gene. He was a practicing example to his crew, illustrating positive attitude, faith, a strong work ethic, intelligence, teamwork, and the idea that one

114

should never stop learning. Confidence is different than being arrogant or being cocky. It's a thin line from what I've witnessed among people throughout my career. Confidence is centered on yourself, what you have control over, and a belief that you can get things done. Confidence is not comparing yourself to other people or blaming others or trying to prove you are better than others. This is where I believe many people go off the path and become viewed by others as being arrogant, selfish, and conceited.

Decision-making and getting input from staff. Jean Luc Picard (better yet, his character), in portraying the modern day "real" Manager, is ultimately responsible for making decisions and taking responsibility. Regardless of how smart Jean Luc's character is, he always consults experts and his leadership team for input. Then, after getting key people's input and recommendations, Jean Luc would make a decision, and he expected everyone under his command to accept it and implement it wholeheartedly. He was never judgmental of someone's comment or recommendation. This allowed for more ideas and open discussions. Jean Luc never "took" over meetings, given his obvious senior rank in meetings. He participated whenever possible. He led a meeting by being a facilitator, not because he was Captain. If urgency is required, he would control the pace of the meeting and run through the agenda more quickly, but he would explain himself enough so everyone understood how and why he was progressing the way he was. When he reached a decision or decided on a recommendation, he would tell his staff to begin implementing the decision with the famous phrase, "make it so".

Treating everyone fairly and with respect. One of the "management" philosophies I admired in the series was the relationship between rank and respect. In the show, regardless of the character's rank, they are all treated as a peer level respect. There is a leadership and command structure hierarchy. However high level characters like the Captain's, Admiral's, and First Officers had the same respect level for their subordinates as they have for their peers. In our current day real world, it is very easy for so many managers to fall into the trap of either using their rank to get everything done and/or living as if they are better than everyone who holds a lesser rank. I also like how in Star Trek, there is never any mention of compensation associated with rank. Nor is money ever needed by leaders to motivate subordinates to perform.

Assuming responsibility and its consequences. Jean Luc's main responsibility, while pursuing the core mission of the USS Enterprise, was to take care of his crew. Similarly, each crewmember was responsible for the well being of fellow crewmembers in pursuit of the same core mission. The lesson which was conveyed in the series was that crew members (aka.

Employees) assumed responsibility for their actions and decisions and its resulting consequences. More subtly, people work as a team; people are not criticized for making mistakes. Any result, good or bad, does not lead to unproductive time wasted on finger pointing and bickering. The crew refocused on what was needed to move forward.

Leadership. Leadership is such a common term used in business and group settings. It's even referred to in Star Trek in various ways. Earning a "command" in Star Trek is getting promoted to a Captain and being given a Starship. There are numerous articles and books written about leadership. Yet, leadership is a squishy (no, this is not a Star Trek term, but it is so descriptive that it just has to be used here) concept to characterize and even more difficult to predict and measure. Watching the series and how Captain Picard is portrayed is worth a thousand words. I won't reinvent the wheel in rewriting what leadership is and how to achieve it. I highly suggest you watch the TV series and read up on the many excellent books and articles describing Leadership. I will repeat and emphasize the point I made earlier about Leadership – many Managers/Executives intermingle confidence, leadership, and power. Managers/Executives behave as if these characteristics are one in the same and this is illustrated best in meetings and the way Manager's make decisions. Many Managers act like the king in meetings. They don't enlist their staff for input and suggestions. They try to take over every meeting, even ones that they are not hosting. These Managers believe this is the way to act as a leader because they want to prove they are confident and smart; that they have to exhibit their high rank (i.e. power). On a primitive level, the feeling of power is addictive. Sadly, they are acting counter-productively with what a Manager needs to do to be successful. Don't fall into this trap. If I had to sum up Leadership, it is the act of being able to influence a person or team towards achieving positive results, positively.

Key Actions Checklist

☐ Talk with pet owners and people with kids about their "management" experience with their pets and/or kids. Watch episodes of *Dog Whisperer* on National Geographic Channel starring Cesar Millan. Victoria Stilwell is another famous dog trainer.

☐ Watch some episodes of *Star Trek: Next Generation and Star Trek: Voyager.* You may just be surprised at how much you can learn from their leadership examples.

116

Chapter 12 – Managing Down

"My main job was developing talent. I was a gardener providing water and other nourishment to our top 750 people. Of course, I had to pull out some weeds, too." ~ Jack Welch

You've been promoted to a manager! Now what?

You've wanted to be a manager for what seems like an entire career (even if most of you are barely 20 something and fresh out of college). Going forward, as you work in corporations, you'll see people who are managers who shouldn't be. And you'll wonder, "Why them? What about me?" Then one day, you get your chance, for whatever reason or circumstance, to be a manager. Maybe you followed the advice in this book and stood out among the herd by specifically doing what was described in the previous few chapters.

In any case, Congratulations! You've broken through a difficult barrier. Welcome to the club. Savor the achievement. Go celebrate because there won't be much time when you start this new career phase.

This is the time to delegate all your work, kickback, and enjoy the big paycheck. NOT!

The good news is you're earning more…a higher salary that is (we hope). Some promotions don't come with a salary increase right away. The other good news is that you cracked the Managerial Glass Ceiling and you are on your way to higher levels in the corporate pyramid.

The sort-of-bad news (only if your expectations were too high) is that lower level management positions (excluding sales management positions) generally do not include any bonus, stock grants, stock options, commissions, or any of those glamorous compensation perks. (Sorry to burst your corporate bubble, but that's the way it is) Your goal is to get into middle management and higher anyway, where the perks start to accelerate and accumulate.

The ugly news is that despite what most non-manager employees think – "managers earn the big bucks"– they're wrong. In fact, lower level managers work harder and make less on an hourly basis. As mentioned earlier in this book, managers have more responsibilities, bigger goals, and are doing it all on a fixed exempt salary status. One final "hardship" – it's lonely at the top and it's lonelier at each higher management level.

If you also recalled in the "Managing Up" chapter, the focus was on supporting your immediate boss/manager to be successful. In "Managing Down," your focus is to create an environment so your staff can successfully "manage up" to you and, in turn, you can be successful managing up by achieving your goals. However, there is a challenge you must face that your boss at the next level faces less of and so forth at each higher level – the lower level employees require much more hand holding, care, and feeding. The lower level employees, and even first line managers/supervisors, don't grasp (and may never grasp) the concepts of "managing up." Thus, it is the trio of challenges – managing up, delivering large goals, and extra managing down efforts – that make the lower and middle management positions such a right of passage to the more lucrative executive levels. When you finally do achieve the higher ranks within your company, you can rest assured that you have earned all of the rewards that come along with it, given that you have worked hard and taken on the trio of challenges.

Although your priority is to manage up, managing down effectively becomes arguably the most vital part of that effort. Remember earlier in this book, a manager must be a people manager because the manager's goals are too big for him/her to achieve alone? Therefore, having people reporting to you makes managing down a necessary evil in order for you to achieve your goals. By the way, people management happens to be the most difficult task for managers.

When my one and only child was born, prior to me becoming a manager, a very bright and more seasoned employee gave me a book as a baby shower gift. The book was entitled, "Children: The Challenge" by Rudolf Dreikurs. Little did I know then that people management would be so similar to raising children, so you can deduce how challenging people management is. That's the reason most of the managing down insights are about people. There are ways you can get through the gauntlet with the help of some insights. The good news is that it's all worth it. It is still better to be in the middle of the herd, than at the back of the herd. But be careful what you wish for!

I've saved the most insightful and core advice about managing people for the next chapter. For this chapter, we'll discuss the general concepts and insights about managing down.

It's all about what bus and what seat

A common analogy used by the managerial world is to describe their department (aka. your team) as a "bus" (like a school bus). I don't know where and why this analogy is used, but I can guarantee you will hear it used in the corporate hallways among managers. The bus itself is the representation of their department and the seats in the bus are the job positions, and the people in the seats are the staff members. Every manager's desire is to have the right people in the right seat on his or her bus.

In layman terms, a manager needs to define what the bus is, where the bus is going, what the seats are, and whether the right person is in the right seat. To translate, the manager must:

- define his or her department.

- define department's goals and how they align with upper management's goals.

- develop tactics to achieve the goals (The first three bullets define what type of bus, where it's going, and how it's getting there).

- determine what the positions are required to implement tactics.

- Put people with the matching skills and talent into the proper positions. (The last two bullets determine the seating arrangement.)

-

What usually challenges a manager in fulfilling the ideal bus model is the reality that most managers inherit a bus with people already in the bus and in certain seats. When this happens, the manager must evolve the department's goals and tactics, resulting in a mismatch with the current staff members and the new skill sets required. Thus you hear the terms, "he/she is in the wrong bus" or "he/she is in the wrong seat of the bus".

Managers must correct this as soon as possible:

- Get your HR representative involved with the revision of job descriptions and reviewing current people on the bus with the job descriptions.

- Get a plan in place (again with the HR person) to communicate the new goals and job requirements.

- Monitor the people against the goals.

- And, as soon as possible, implement a plan to move people to a new seat or off your bus. Your HR person can assist with available options that would include: training, transferring to another department/bus, transitioning to a new job/seat, or being dismissed/laid-off/off the bus station.

Forewarning: this is not an easy process because most companies do not have the stomach for most of these tactics, despite what your boss or what the company leaders' eager rhetoric is. Thus, the suggestions are to start early, get HR involved, communicate regularly with the affected people, be professional, be fair, and be respectful. However, if you don't get this part right, you will spend the majority of your time "baby sitting," dealing with poor performers, and working on disciplinary activities. This also doesn't include all the explaining you will have to do with your executives about why you are not hitting your goals. (Not fun.)

Hire or Grow a stable of "A", "B", and "C" Players

Labeling staff members with an A-F rating ("A" being the highest) is a common practice among managers and HR professionals in the corporate world. Going back to the bus model, just because you have a person who fits the right seat, the person can still range from a fair performer to an exceptional performer. In an ideal world, you want to have a department of all "A" players. But that's not realistic. As hard as you may try to hire the right person or evolve staff members to be an "A" player, most will not turn out to be top performers.

Top performers, aka "A" players, are rare. A true "A" player can and will exceed the job description and excel at achieving the job goals in the most professional manner (meaning that getting the job is not good enough if it isn't done in the right way (Chapter 7), such that the person will easily become over-qualified for the position. But you need these players because they will help you reach and exceed your goals for several years. Your role is to develop them and keep them motivated long enough to help you and, in turn, you need to help them move on to greater opportunities.

"B" players are good to have in the department because they are good performers. They get the job done sometimes better than expected. They will occasionally show flashes of "A" attributes (creative, overachiever, resourceful, leadership, mastering hard and soft skills). A few "C" players are also good to have in the department. "C" players are the workhorses because they perform most of the routine tasks in the department and have little ambition to progress in their career. "C" players are predictable and generally consistent at what they do. Conversely, don't expect "C" players to overachieve or exceed your expectation. They neither have the skills or desire.

As the manager, you need to cultivate the potential "A" players among the "B" and "C" people while motivating the current "A" players to perform their magic. One method advocated by some is the "Bottom 10% rule": that is to continually work out the bottom 10% performers in your department.

I have found that this can work, with a few caveats:

- Your company must support this (translate: have the stomach for it). Firing people takes time, but the bigger issue is the risk the corporation takes on given all the rules and games employees play when they are "let go."

- By chance, you may have a fairly high performing group that has little standard deviation between the highest and lowest performers. In these cases, even the low performers are probably better than their peers in the marketplace. The effort and risk is probably not worth the benefits of gaining a few more "A" players.

- There is a risk to having too many "A" players. You can dilute the motivation among the "A" players when they realize they are not getting as much attention and there are fewer opportunities. I found that this to be especially true in many departments with transactional functions. In these cases, there is nothing wrong with having a lot of average performers that get the job done, done well, and at respectable speed and volume.

A quick note about hiring in general – there are as many books and seminars available about hiring and interviewing people as there are about how to get hired and how to interview. I encourage you to read as many as you can. There are many condensed articles on the Internet. Many companies have internal classes and/or will pay you to attend external ones. I do have one final comment in light of my discussions above about "A" players, wrong bus passengers, and the unprecedented unemployment the country is experiencing – be very leery of job candidates who were previously laid off from medium/large corporations. I know this sounds heartless but, as I mentioned earlier, poor performers were often the first to be let go during a layoff event. I caution you to really dig in to make sure you are not hiring a problem employee. Reference checks are useful. Checking out social networks and blogs are revealing. For example, a cynical person will be cynical throughout their lives, not just at work.

Motivating your employees

There are countless books and information on this subject, so I am not going to spend a lot of words repeating them. I will touch on a few because it is relevant to certain topics, mostly in the upcoming chapters of this book. This is a useful topic to master, so I strongly encourage you to do your research. Motivating people is not as simple as you may think.

I will leave you with a few things I've learned and practiced successfully about motivating employees:

- Golden rule: start with people that have motivation. Short of this, no one has magic advice. It's like trying to change someone's personality; it's just not easy to do.

- Money is not the primary motivator. Everyone expects to be paid. Additional dollars won't get you additional motivation. It's not linear and there's little long-term correlation. To use money effectively, use it in a surprise manner and tie it to an achievement or preferred behavior.

- Treating staff members with respect, trust, care, and fairness will help you achieve loyalty and that leads to motivated members.

- Create an environment people want to be a part of; they will be more motivated people.

- Getting to be friends with your staff members is not a motivational technique. Earning their respect is more effective than earning their friendship. There are more negative issues than positive ones when bosses become friends with their staff members. (The term "be their parent not their best friend" is often used to refer to a mother or father who tries to be their child's friend rather than a respected authority figure. Thus, "be their boss not their best friend" is a useful saying when it comes to gaining the respect of your employees.)

Surround yourself with people smarter than you

The operative words are "surround" and "smart". In the corporate world, "smart" also means diverse. Diverse is the new "smart." Diverse more aptly describes the elements of corporate smart: knowledge, experience, intellect, abilities, skills, and so on. You'll be surprised how many managers do not or cannot "surround" themselves with "smart" people. Managers, like people, feel threatened if they are not the smartest in the room or if they are with people they are not comfortable with. The latter can be due to the manager's ignorance of someone's culture, language, lifestyle, etc.

It makes sense when you think about the typical make up of managers and of human beings. They are Alpha Dogs. They like staff members agreeing with them. The "emperor with no clothes syndrome" is commonplace in the corporate world. Managers don't like to feel threatened or inferior to someone who is smarter, but more importantly someone else who might get the credit. Sadly, many managers are unfamiliar or uncomfortable with people that are culturally different from them. Perhaps, even sadder still, is that these insecurities are not myths. A smart, diverse staff will help you excel in your goals. Corporate leaders view strongly a manager's ability to assembly, build, and/or groom such capable team members.

Apply your operating system

Remember the discussion about a manager's operating system in Chapter 8 – "Managing Up"? As the manager now, you have an obligation to share your operating system with your staff.

And make sure you set the basics with each employee:

- Have clear, measurable goals in place with each employee, communicated and assigned early. I believe every manager learns the common acronym for setting SMART goals: **S**pecific, **M**easurable, **A**ppropriate, **R**ealistic, and **T**ime-limit.

- Require a plan from the employee on how they will achieve the goals. I stress the word "how". Poor performance extends beyond simply reaching a goal. The manner an employee goes about achieving the goal and how he/she behaves are performance elements. For example: Was a plan developed well? Was the plan managed and implemented well? Were project team members satisfied with the employee's interaction?

- Get regular updates from the employee of their progress to their plan and towards their goals. Hold them accountable. "Keep the spotlight on them" as a business saying goes. Studies have found that employees are more productive if they believe people are watching what they are doing. Metaphorically, the "light" reveals what they are doing compared to not seeing what they are doing if they were in the "dark." It is perfectly fine to apply a different, more active operating system for employees on a performance notice.

- Address shortcomings immediately when the employee deviates from their plan.

- Finally, just as cows can't change their spots, people can't change their spots either (personality and characteristic "spots"). Many of us managers have tried only to learn the hard way that it just doesn't happen.

Trust your staff, but record, monitor and follow up with their progress

Fact is people are people, as I've stated throughout the book. Your staff, therefore, will predictably make mistakes, forget things, get behind in their schedule, experiencing setbacks, and may even be conscientiously avoiding to tell you something, etc. Trust is earned and that takes time. You will have different levels of trust for each staff member based on the type of job function, the member's experience level, and your own experience with each member. However, different trust levels do NOT mean you treat them differently. You have to keep your interaction with each person consistent.

Go back to the operating system you and your staff has agreed to and make sure the operating system has checks and balances with respect to when and how progress is to be reported and how follow up occurs. Hold people, especially your staff, accountable. I highly recommend you have a practice of keeping track of action items and assignments that will automatically flag a reminder to you to follow up with those actions and assignments you delegated to staff members. If you leave it up to your staff to keep you updated, all the time, in a timely fashion, you are smoking some drug. As an example of a practice, I kept an action list from meetings (staff meetings, project meetings, task force meetings, etc.) that were always reviewed at the beginning of each regularly scheduled follow-on meeting. I also kept a delegation list on my calendar application (MS Outlook or Mac iCalendar) with follow-up dates to remind me to check in with the particular staff member if I hadn't heard anything. My staff knew I was not going to forget a delegated item so they could not just "fly under the radar" and ignore it. They also knew I kept a record so I could hold people who consistently missed assignments accountable.

Are there different approaches for managing different generational employee?

The general answer is "no", despite what many books and articles will have you believe. I do agree and have experienced that there are ways to be more effective, but that can be said about any human being, not because they are from different generations.

My experience and golden rules about effectively working or managing all people are the same:

- Be courteous and polite. Everyone appreciates being treated in a courteous manner.

- Give praise and recognition. Everyone appreciates getting a "thank you" for good work.

- Show respect for the experiences a person has. It doesn't matter how old or young they are. Everyone has experiences and talent they bring to the team. Even enthusiasm is a valuable talent that helps a team and company. Enthusiasm is not age-based.

- Show respect to people's likes and dislikes. Nobody likes being put down for what they represent or what they enjoy. It's one in the same, isn't it? People extend their image and self through what they do, what they like, and what they associate with. For example, you may not like rap, but you should not put it down. Be open to understanding why someone would like it. And if you cannot understand and "you don't have anything nice to say, it's better to say nothing at all", as a very insightful person said long ago, which still holds true today.

- Lead by example and with integrity. People will treat you the way you treat others. Put another way, people will work with and for you the way you work with and/or manage them.

Yes, these are pretty common sense aren't they? They are when you are reading them. It's amazing how many people forget or don't practice them. Perhaps these behaviors are not so common. Or maybe they are just not common in the corporate world. If a person was not brought up with these "common sense" behaviors, then these behaviors are foreign and not natural.

I've read many articles and books on this subject. I've attended numerous seminars and it's true there are tips and techniques to improve the effectiveness of working and/or managing people of different generations. No doubt there are differences between Baby Boomers (born between 1950-1970), Generation X (between 1960's-1980), Generation Y or Millennium Generation (between 1970's-2000), and the Generation Z or iGeneration (between 1990's to present). Some differences are obvious; music, fashion, slang, entertainment, technology, approach to life, stage of life, so on. I suggest you review these articles and research on your own. I'm a huge proponent of continuous learning and connecting the dots (if it isn't obvious by now!). Learning about differences in people improves your interaction with a broad range people types and ages. Studies in generational differences will help you in business beyond people interaction, such as in marketing and sales. Strictly as far as this section's topic and questions are concerned, I've found that before you spend your time with all those tips and techniques, your foundation behavior must be built on the golden rules above. They will take you far, even if you never employ special tips.

Managing poor performers...off the seat or bus

Managing poor performers is the worst part of being a manager for many reasons. Golden rule: Get your HR person involved early. Then proceed with the following:

Firstly, there is a lot of non-productive work involved. It's like a criminal court of law – you have to prove to the employee and the company that the employee is a poor performer. That means you have to gather the evidence. This includes documenting all their failures, all their improvement plans, all their interim progress reports, all the meetings notes, all the history such as previous annual performance reviews, etc. And speaking of improvement plans, you have to write it. Then there's all the time you spend meeting with the employee to go over it. None of these activities produce a product or service your company can sell to generate sales and revenue – totally non-productive.

Second, there is the distraction and opportunity cost to your time and attention while you are trying to make your goals. While you're spending all your time with the poor performers, the good performers don't get your time. It's the old public school trap – always catering to the lowest performers and thus not spending the time to develop the stars.

Lastly, there's all the emotional stress and drama. Staff members will cry, scream, threaten, go silent, and so on. Discussing bad news and providing criticism is no fun for you or the receiving employee. I've never experienced a "good" constructive criticism session.

There are a lot of seminars, internal classes, and papers written about managing poor performers. There are differences among companies and state laws. I encourage you to do your homework.

Your staff are not your buddies

Earlier in this book, there was a discussion about being "lonely at the top". This statement is not just physical but figurative. "Lonely" does not mean being physically isolated. As a manager, you will still have physical contact, but figuratively speaking you really are alone because the socialization is limited and guarded and....lonely.

You have to build professional relationships WITHOUT resorting to socializing with your staff members. Many managers treat both as the same. It is not. It's true a manager should build a relationship with their staff members. Doing so involves some amount of time together and the quality/content of that time spent. Use discretion in choosing the time, activity, and conversations. Keep all three business-oriented and as professional as possible. Earning respect as a manager does not require you to become best friends or buddies with your staff member. I've seen young managers host weekend poker parties at their homes for some staff members, then talking about it in public at work in the hallway and coffee room the following Monday. Only male staff members were invited and there was alcohol involved. There are so many things wrong with this scenario. You risk showing favoritism to some, thus creating distrust and animosity among your staff. Worst of all, you may create a harassment situation. Finally, you will cloud your judgment of employees, especially when you have to dish out assignments, poor performance reviews, and criticism.

Is it all bad? No, but you need to be aware and act accordingly. There's a lot at risk ranging from harassment to career limiting to reducing your leadership aura.

A piece of advice on how to conduct myself as a manager was given to me early in my management days, that actually took several years to truly understand, came from a VP who said, "it is best to be thick skinned and project a sterile, almost cold personality". He also said, "management is not a popularity contest." Sound advice. The immature manager believes becoming best friends or being the popular person or being the center of attention are ways to rally their staff around them to get things done. It may feel like it works, but it is a false front, at best, and becomes a slippery slope before you know it. Many employees act selfishly and "kiss up" to their management by being yes-people and will do anything they feel the manager would like. It's all a farce. Don't learn the hard way.

Devil's Advocate

See Chapter 8, but now you get to apply the same approach down to your staff members. It's a great way to keep them on their toes, challenge their innovation, and push their professional envelope.

Key Actions Checklist

☐ Read the book, *Children: The Challenge* by Rudolf Dreikurs.

☐ Take seminars, classes, and conferences on managing and motivating people. Read books and articles. Talk with your mentors.

☐ Identify the Alpha Dogs among your organization.

☐ Communicate your operating system clearly to your staff.

☐ Develop a system that will effectively assist you in holding people accountable by following up with people and delegated tasks.

☐ You and your staff should attend a personality assessment class such as Myers-Briggs or DISC.

☐ Practice SMART goal setting. Be diligent about documenting your staff's performance especially those performing poorly.

Chapter 13 – Networking

"It's not what you know, but who you know."

~ English Proverb, Unknown

You've all heard this saying before. The implication is that it doesn't matter how smart you are or how much you know, if you do not have the opportunity to use your brilliance. People open doors, therefore, who-you-know (more than the what-you-know) will provide the opportunities. To add an element of speed, I would suggest a slight change to the saying: If you want to get ahead in the corporate herd, sooner, "it's *what* you know AND <u>who</u> you know".

Most the book so far discussed the what-you-need-to-know part. This chapter is the who-you-know part, which is better known as Networking.

"Networking" is one of those concepts I believe a lot of young people do not understand how to practice, just like the concept of "respect." The latter will be another story.

The purpose of networking is to extend your people connections by tapping into their connections, and so on. It is achieved through people who can directly or indirectly lead to countless opportunities, which will help you in business and life. The possible benefits are endless, many being unexpected. What is known is that the more people you are connected to, the pool of connections increases exponentially and opportunities present themselves more readily.

Networking is…awkward

If you place networking on a social continuum, it would land somewhere between selling and dating. Aren't most people uncomfortable with both of these scenarios? Like selling and dating, you have to initiate the first connection and, likely, most of the follow-on contacts. That alone is awkward enough. And just like selling and dating, it is so awkward to play the game and dance around the obvious desired end result – you want the person to buy what you have to sell or to accept a date with you. But people don't work that way. People are not good at being direct and people don't like rejection. So we do the dance.

Same thing happens in networking. No one simply says, "Hi, I would like you to be in my network circle, okay?" or "Will you go out of your way to uncover opportunities for me?" Just like asking someone to marry you at the first introduction doesn't work either. People "buy" from each other based on their comfort with the other person. And comfort is built on relationships. Relationships are built on trust. And trust is generally built over time and on actions, not just words. Wow. No wonder people, especially young people, have a tough time with this.

I watch my daughter struggle with this concept. She's very personable and she's an extrovert. She has over 500 friends on Facebook! Yet, I see her struggle with the true concept and practice of networking; sadly I believe she is in the majority with other young people. Most people struggle with understanding how to network and even more people struggle with the practice of networking – cultivating the relationship. It's not good enough that you understand the concept; you have to make the effort. Admittedly, I struggled with it.

Like it or not, you are all in Sales

Let's get this point on the table… for everyone who wants to mooove ahead, you must embrace the Sales process. To mooove ahead, you have to sell your brand, your ideas, your candidacy for promotions, and so on.

It all starts with making contact. The most difficult part of networking is getting the nerve to meet new people. This is analogous to the Sales concept called cold-calling; introducing yourself to companies who do not know you and are not currently doing business with you. Sales people have to cold call because this is one of the only ways to increase sales and for companies to increase market share. You have to become more comfortable with meeting people you do not know because this is how you increase your networking market share. As mentioned way back in Chapter 2, being successful in Sales is based on a numbers game. Sales people are taught; you make 100 cold-calls to get 10 appointments. And for every 10 appointments, you will likely get one sale. The point is, if you make enough cold-calls, the sales process will work out eventually to an average, predictable number of sales. BUT, if you make zero cold-calls, you will make a predictable ZERO sales. The more people you meet and connect with, the larger your networking pool gets and the greater the number of possible opportunities.

Networking How-to's

- Populate your network. There's no network without people, so meet as many people as you can. I think I drove this point pretty hard in the previous section. The bottom line is: put yourself in positions to meet new people.

- Record & Organize your network. Don't pass judgment about people you meet. You should be like a reporter, taking note of their basic information and recording it – name, occupation, and contact info (a business card would be great). Note them in your contact book. In today's world of smartphones, PCs, laptops, tablets, and so forth, you should have your contacts in some electronic form. Get a business card scanning app so you can efficiently record the contact info into your system. A personal contact system organizes records and facilitates the addition of notes, so that you can then recall useful information about the person. Besides basic contact information, you will want to note such things as where and when you met, who introduced you, what are their interests, etc. This will assist with your relationship building.

- Diversify your network. My daughter may have over 500 facebook friends, but 97% of them are about her same age (between 19-23). She's missing out on the whole point of networking – it's not all about quantity...quality counts big-time. How is she going to tap into opportunities, learn about new things, get advice about a broad set of topics, and get different perspectives from fellow 20 year olds? It's like the blind-leading-the-blind. The only way to meet people of different ages, different cultures, and different social classes is to extend outside of her social, professional, and cultural circles. Some of the best places to meet people who can be useful in your network are social circles (such as charities, fund-raisers), and clubs (such as Bridge Clubs or Tennis Clubs). The bonus for meeting people in these settings is that now you have something in common that transcends age, social, financial and professional barriers. Having something in common is a key in developing relationships and trust, which will be discussed several paragraphs later.

- Do the above quickly. The faster you build your diverse network, the faster you can develop the relationships and tap into opportunities your network may provide.

- It's all about relationships. Building relationships with people is to find common interest and to stay in touch over periods of time.

There is no strict formula to this. I wish it was as simple as meeting a stranger, realizing you both have a shared interest in mountain biking, and the person becomes comfortable enough to buy whatever product from you at any price at that first meeting. It rarely works that way. All that being said, your goal and approach is to find something in common. Sports like football and golf are associated with business because most of the corporate world is still led by men and the majority of men like sports, especially football and golf. When I worked in the Bay Area (Northern California), starting a conversation with, "how about those '9ers?" always worked to build a rapport.

- Give more than you take. Trust, the heart of a relationship, is built through exchanges. Offering something does not mean giving a person money. It can be some suggestions or advice. For example, you share a great website with a person or you refer a great consultant or contractor. You can offer to introduce them to someone that could help her/his business or who can help her/him solve a problem. Just having a good, meaningful, enlightening conversation is a gift and a great way to build trust with someone. It's a strange thing about human beings; some will often connect trust with enjoying a person's company. In sales, there's a saying, "People don't necessarily buy the company or the product or the price. People buy from people." It's about building trust and a relationship.

- Relationship is built over time. Relationship is the investment of time and effort you put in to cultivate those contacts in your networking pool. Everyone has a busy life and trying to keep tabs with even a few people and spend quality time to develop the relationship is much harder to do then it appears. I found this to be an area many people experience failure in their networking effort. You're not just connecting with one person, but to their circle of contacts (a.k.a. their network). Networking takes some time and effort to cultivate, especially with key people who might be highly influential, highly inspirational, or well connected. If you do not regularly see or talk with these people, you need to make it a point to stay in touch. I recommend putting reminders in your calendar (your software calendar, of course) to send an email, make a phone call, send a text, or arrange a lunch. When you see or hear something that might be related or be of interest to that person, send them the article or an email about whatever it was that reminded you of her/him. THIS IS THE KEY TO

NETWORKING – Keeping in touch and NOT asking for something. In fact, the more you can offer the easier it will be when you do need help to ask for it. In a social circle, it's a lot easier because you don't want anything. In business, you are usually not socializing with everyone. It might turn into a social relationship, but the real truth is that you really do want something! Therefore, you have to develop the relationship in more deliberate, seemingly more awkward way. You have to be more active in creating the opportunities to get together, how to carry a conversation, share, learn about each other, and develop trust.

Young people think they have nothing to offer in professional networking relationships. That's true to a large extent. However, young people can offer their knowledge of current technologies such as social networking and consumer electronics, such as iPhone tips.

Take advantage of a human trait – people love to be asked for advice and treated as the "wise-person". Whether it's because people like their ego's stroked or they enjoy the psychological returns of helping others or both, this is a useful approach to networking.

Young people can build up their "asset and offerings". Increase your knowledge and experience by learning and trying out many diverse things. Remember the advice early in this book…here's where the dots all start to connect and become useful in many ways. Your knowledge becomes an asset.

Your network becomes an asset too. You can use your network to help others, to get information for people and, in turn, you may be offering something useful back to the network. This whole Eco-system works organically and starts to grow itself!

Tony's Stories

I was recently reminded of how far I've come with my network, even though I started practicing the principles above relatively late in my career. It's still not as natural for me as for some people. Lucky for me (or unlucky, depending upon how you look at it), I was rarely in a position where I had to leverage my network. At least that's what I thought until I looked back and realized my most profound career milestones were all due to people in my network. I was lucky. Or was I? Just imagine what opportunities may have presented itself if I had practiced networking better. I mean, I worked in Silicon Valley in the early formative years. How many people did I meet (co-workers, friends of friends) that have gone on to prominent positions? I have learned that several have started successful high tech companies or become Presidents of several companies.

To keep things in perspective, I am reminded of how much I have done in developing my network. One of my tennis friends recently asked me how I know so many people in so many walks of life. My answer was three fold – 1) I made it an effort to get involved in lots of activities, clubs, and groups; 2) I made it an effort to get involved in diverse activities; and 3) I force myself to meet people at those activities. Upon comparison, my friend did not do any of the items in my answer. He did not get involved with activities. He mostly interacted with the same small circle of friends and the same few activities. Even within the tennis circle, he confined himself to a small circle of tennis people. During a discussion about a college tennis rule change, he was impressed to learn that I not only knew the actual reason for the rule change, but I cited that my source was a former University of Southern California tennis coach who was on the NCAA Tennis rules committee. The coach and I were members of a local tennis club. During the same discussion session, we switched topic and started talking about the upcoming 3rd generation Toyota Prius plug-in because we both own a 2nd generation Prius. I shared some information about the Prius I learned from my friend who at Toyota. I met this friend while doing charity work at the school both our daughters attended.

From my friend's perspective, I would view myself as being successful at networking. However in my view, the two stories above point out lost opportunities, because I did not practice networking early and to the extent I could have when I finally did. What if I had recorded and stayed in touch with all those people in Silicon Valley? And for those people I did meet and recorded after I realized what networking was, what if I spent more effort cultivating them…would more opportunities have surfaced? How many opportunities did I really miss out on simply because I didn't know the ins and outs of networking from the get-go?

Key Actions Checklist

☐   Get involved in different social, professional, and cultural circles in order to build a large, diverse network.

☐   Incorporate the use of a contact manager software application.

☐ Develop a method of reminding yourself to touch bases with key people in your network AND a practice of relationship building. Use a calendar application.

Chapter 14 – Myth Busters

"The pure and simple truth is rarely pure and never simple."

~ Oscar Wilde (1854-1900) Irish poet and dramatist.

We will close out with a potpourri of provocative topics and myths that people don't normally want to talk about in the corporate world. We're not going to stick our heads in the sand to avoid topics just because they're sensitive. The corporate world has its good, bad, and ugly realities. You need to be aware of them and how to deal with them if you want to advance easily.

You don't have to worry about the Race card

When I was writing this book, I seriously thought about using a pen name that was more "American" instead of my Asian name as the author. If you're not a minority, you probably don't truly understand how powerful perception and stereotype is. Go to any large bookstore and walk through the "Business and Management" aisle. Do you see any Business or Management books by an Asian author? I didn't. (For that matter, how about Indian, Hispanic, or Persian?) And if there is one, I don't believe it has ever risen to any iconic level. Lucky for the African Americans, people cannot tell if an author is African-American since they were given Caucasian/European surnames.

Are there no Asians in Business and Management? Can't Asians write? Are Asians no good at Business and Management? Are Asian's holding out on sharing their Business and Management knowledge? Regardless, the result is the same: there is a perception that Asians are not the image of business or management leaders. If I use my real name, would this book be discounted based on those perceptions? That was my fear. I toyed with "American" pen names. How about Tony K. Peters, Seth K. Goodwin, Tony D. Smith, T. K. Rosenbloom?

Depending on where you work, you are likely a minority. How do you conform if you're a different breed of cow from the rest of the herd? Are Holstein cows better than Jersey cows? Outside of cosmetic surgery, there's little you can change in appearance and body dimension.

Here are suggestions on how to make the most of your minority situation:

Be you. Work with what you are born with. There are advantages to being different, such as the fact that it may be easier for people to remember you. You work so hard at standing out of the herd through your accomplishments; you already have built-in visibility because you are different. Profiling and stereotypes can work to your advantage. For example, Asians are thought to be very technical and generally "smarter". If you're Asian and you are not that smart, people will think you are. That's not a bad trait. Asians look younger, so at 50 years old, you can compete for jobs because you look 35. On the flip side, Asians are supposed to be weak in the interpersonal skills area and considered passive. Take advantage of your stereotyped strength traits and improve or overcome your pre-determined weakness traits. In short, make the stereotypes work for you, not against you.

Location. Work for a corporation or location where you are not a minority or where there is more acceptance. For example, California and Washington State, and their respective business communities, have large populations of Asians and Middle-Easterners.

Be good at what you do. People in business are color-blind to the color green – color of money that is. In other words, if you are good at what you do, you are bringing value and success to your managers/corporations and that's the color (and nationality) they will see. I was inspired by the movie starring Will Smith based on a true story, *The Pursuit of Happiness,* because one of the triumphs in the movie was how the character Smith portrayed was one of the early African American employees at a major Pacific Stock Exchange brokerage firm in the early 1970's. A major message of the movie – *What you have control over is you and how hard you work.* Some things you can't change, such as the fact that most American corporations are lead by tall white males or whatever the majority is at your location. There is nothing wrong with working a little harder to be better at your job. It's not fair that you have to work harder, but that's life. Stop fretting. Change what you can. Besides, won't you want to err on working hard to get results and being tired vs. rested, but still not succeeding? Plus, as an added bonus – having to work harder will ultimately lead to gaining more experience, having a stronger work ethic, and achieving a higher level of knowledge about your company.

Change your identity. People form stereotypes about people before they even meet them based on a name, reputations, or job function, etc. Changing your name is certainly one tactic that has impact because your name is used in many places. It identifies you. Often people know your name before they meet you in person. Stereotypes form without you even being present to defend or reinforce them. Movie stars are examples of people who understand that image is everything, thus the reason for so many in Hollywood that have changed their names.

A few stories illustrating the impact of a name:

- Ask my wife. She's 98% Caucasian but she noticed how differently people treated her before and after they met her in person just because her married name changed from Green to Wong.

- I have a good friend, John Lee, who is Caucasian and born in Kansas. He married a Japanese woman named Ann Endo. Ann never uses her married name professionally (it would be Ann Lee). She explains it was because she did not want people she did business with to pre-judge her as an Asian by her name before they met in person. I got a kick that she kept her Japanese surname because it sounded more American than her Caucasian husband's surname!?

- At one of my employers, I learned from the HR Representative a year after I was hired as the Customer Support Director that I almost did not get hired. Her boss, the HR manager, did not want to forward my resume to the hiring VP because the HR manager did not believe an Asian person could have the interpersonal skills necessary to interact effectively with the mostly Caucasian customer base. I'll bet the HR manager would not have pre-judged me if my name was Tony Smith.

You don't have to change your name. I imagine many of you would not do this out of respect for your family name or you don't want to deal with the hassles involved with a name change. Therefore, you need to build a reputation and image for people who have not meet you.

Some suggestions:

- Obviously the brand you've constructed will become the word of mouth from people you've worked with, for, or worked for you, including vendors and industry contacts.

- Make sure your social and professional networks have the information and image you want to project. Take care in what you put and communicate on your facebook, Linked-In, Tweeter, job sites, etc. This is why you want to take care of what these sites have about you very early on. The Internet is so important to a person or company's reputation today, that there are even services to repair or enhance your reputation on the Internet.

- Communicate in advance with people you will be meeting or interacting and craft the communication to paint the image you want these people to have. Again, what brand are you trying to convey? Do the perceptions of you tend to be one of an organized person, detailed oriented, proactive, etc.? Then the communications you put out should reflect it. As an example, your "proactiveness" will be demonstrated by your several emails before the meeting accompanied with an agenda, directions to the meeting location, suggested hotels in the area, reminder email, and so on.

Conform. If you want to get ahead, you stand a much better chance if you fit in with the business environment around you. Fitting in is not solely based on physical appearance. It's the way you act, behave, communicate, etc. Don't give people a chance to confirm their stereotype about you by playing right into their stereotypes. I mentioned how an HR manager in the late 1990's thought Asians had poor interpersonal skills or would not "fit in" with good 'old boy Caucasian customers. Over the years I worked hard on interpersonal skills so I did not sound or act like I "just came off the boat". My wife, USA born and a self-professed Heinz 57 variety Caucasian, is a stickler for proper English. She did not hesitate to correct me whenever she heard my broken English or when I need to enunciate better. I did my homework to learn something about each customer's situation, background, and interest. People become blind to the physical differences with people who have similar interest as theirs. A great place to see this demonstrated is at clubs and organizations where everyone rallies around a common interest or cause.

I'm sure some of you reading this by now are feeling a bit offended that I am recommending you "sell out" your culture or race to get ahead. The traditionalists cite the destruction of their race and culture. Some people go as far as to be militant about acting and sounding too White or too American or too whatever is considered dominant. I'm not here to debate whether conforming is giving into historical wrongs, or whitewashing native cultures, etc. Strictly from a pragmatic perspective of wanting to move ahead in the herd, it seems to me it's all about choice. It's a choice where you want to work, what work you want to do, and whether you want to perform what the environment is comfortable with and desires.

Project a different image. This is a follow on to the topic of "conform." Conform or create your style, but base it on where you are today and what makes you, you. You will need to take inventory of yourself. For this, you need to get help from others so you can define it from their point of view. Then you need to decide what image you want to project. Either you integrate the trait or you learn to be very good at acting it when you are around the work environment. For example, Asians are stereotyped as quiet and cerebral, so learn to be more outspoken, confident, and social. Women are stereotyped as not being as sports oriented, so learn about football, baseball, and golf. Go take some golf lessons. Join a fantasy baseball or football league. Read the sport pages.

Tony's Stories

Unfortunately, this is a true story about a choice that prevented this person from getting ahead. I inherited a 30years old Hispanic employee when I first joined a certain company back in the late 1990's. This employee was frustrated because he could not get promoted. I reviewed his performance records and I told him that he was a good, loyal performer and gave him much of the advice I've put in this book. I stressed one very important requirement of his job – improve his communications skills; be more professional and clear. He did not understand until I recorded his voice during our conversations and played it back. He never noticed (or cared to change) how heavy his Hispanic accent was. It would have been fine if he was dealing with Hispanic customers, but he wasn't. Interestingly (and sadly), he was born in the US and was educated in the Los Angeles school system, but sounded like he just recently migrated here from Mexico.

You can balance work and personal life

Can you really balance work and non-work life? This is probably the second toughest question to answer behind "what's the meaning of life?" Short answer is "sort-of." Long answer is "probably not" because balance is a moving target. It means different things to different people. And it means different things, at different times.

Work and life balance is something that is redefined with each new stage of your life. People in their 20's are generally not married and have all the time in the world to work and play. Then people get married and have kids. Suddenly, they didn't have all the time in the world to work extra hours; in short, priorities changed. Each stage of our lives brings new challenges that define what work and life balance means.

Balance sounds like you can achieve some win-win. You really don't. You're really trying to achieve the best lose-lose. Perhaps the word "balance" should be replaced with the word "sacrifice."

Why write such a long section on this seemingly useless and abstract topic? After all, young people are not concerned with what's going to happen 10, 15, 20 years from now. Absolutely true, however for the few of you that truly want to know what all the future potholes are in order to avoid them and get ahead sooner (in the corporate world and in life), I would be remiss if I did not discuss this topic.

The essential points are:

- You create the balance.

- You choose the tradeoffs (compromises, sacrifices, etc.).

- Make sure you can live with your choices.

- Finally, prioritize doing things so you will not have regrets later.

I'm amazed at all the articles and books that make it sound so easy to achieve balance. They're all advocating giving up something. There's that "sacrifice" thing again. For example, they focus on time management techniques: say "no" more often, touch something only once, organize your office more efficiently, so forth. All these tips center on saving time. Time is a key asset to manage and conserve. With enough time (and money), you can do anything; at least that's the theory.

But it's more than just time; geography and life style come into play. And, unfortunately, you cannot practically save enough time to overcome geography and life style sacrifices. You also cannot make up lost time. For example, take the popular notion by younger people to justify why they should sacrifice everything for work: "I'll have time for that when I'm older." This train of thought misses the concept of lost time and what life is going to be like in the future. There are many things you cannot do or do well when you are older compared to when you are younger. When you finally have time for the activity, the activity is not available to you anymore. When you realize this, you cannot turn back the hands of time. You've forfeited those experiences, and you cannot ever get them back.

Anyone with desires to move ahead will need to relocate as part of their career path. Here's one of the career choices many people have to make (many times over, in some cases). When that great position and promotion is in Iowa or the middle of China, or some place very uncomfortable and foreign, you're pressed to take it because 1) you don't believe there are other options and 2) you don't know if promotional opportunities will present themselves again. You will gain new experiences from making the choice to move, but you also give up experiences. Is it worth the time away from friends and family? Is it worth moving your family around? Nearly all the executives I've worked for have moved 5-7 times in their career. It's all been about their career, at the sacrifice of their own personal interest and their family. But hey, they've provided for their families very well and many are set for a nice retirement. They'll have time for all that other stuff later…when they're older, right? Maybe.

Many of the books and articles give advice about prioritizing and, essentially, giving up something to achieve balance. Sure, it's easy to achieve balance this way if you are prepared to give up a lot. The more you give up, the easy it is to achieve balance. Simple concept. Taking it to the extreme, why not just give up everything except eating, sleeping, and working. That's the trick isn't it? The reality is that life outside of work is made up of way more than just two or three things. And it'll be really easy if you can perfectly define what you REALLY can give up, THEN accept the trade-offs 100% wholeheartedly. Wow, if you can do all this with no guilt, anxiety, or no enduring feelings of being deprived….you are a saint. Since we're human, most of us should work on learning how to deal with the compromise. It helps to have some insight and advance understanding, just so that you are not shocked.

I always find it interesting to meet a 50 or 60 years old person who WAS a mid or upper level manager/Executive but not anymore for whatever reason. They appear lost because their life is not occupied with work. They've associated and depended on work to define and fill their lives so much, they're empty with it. They also talk about what they missed out on because their earlier life was so pre-occupied by their work. They generally concede they would have "smelled the roses" more if they knew they would succeed, because now that they've "succeeded", they cannot go back in time.

Speaking of smelling the roses, the most important "rose" is family. Young people cannot comprehend or care about this topic, but be forewarned, most of you will have a family and you will be faced with choices of how you much time you spend with your family. Family (and friendships) takes cultivation, over time. Many people miss this concept.

This discussion wasn't meant to discuss how to live life and get philosophical. I felt it is important to discuss this concept of balance in the context of this book – which is about helping you to move ahead in the herd. You see, this book does not talk about how far ahead. There are many factors you cannot control that determines how far ahead and how fast, but one factor you can control is to decide when enough is enough.

Here are some road signs to raise your consciousness as you embark on your upward path through the herd:

- Despite the compensation increases as you move ahead in the herd, life doesn't come easier because you make more money. There is work involved…work keeping whatever is important going (kids, friends, hobbies, etc). Understand that your work responsibilities increase as you advance….a manager's work increases exponentially. Did you think that they're giving you more money to do an easier job

- Career advancements impact your life beyond work hours. As mentioned, there is relocation. How do you measure that impact? There is increase in travel which means even less time at home. How do you measure that impact and the non-work activity opportunities lost? And how do you measure the mental time work occupies which goes well beyond work hours…just look at the Smartphone handcuff. You're working all the time, not just 8-5.

- Making money is a huge gravitational pull…but do you know how much is enough? Have you thought about opportunity cost of time vs. the incremental monies you pile up?

- You give up time and age…tough to put a price on that.

You shouldn't job hop around companies

The days of working for the same company for 30 years and retiring is the stuff of legend. It just doesn't happen today very often. In fact, the transition began happening in the late 1980's. You can name on one hand the industries or jobs where you can (and should) spend your entire career and retire at: public jobs such as teachers and municipal employees; union-driven jobs such as dockworkers, grocery clerks. That's about it.

Notice most of these jobs are blue-collar jobs and many are trade jobs. Not many corporate industries. Those environments put a penalty for changing organizations. For the remaining jobs in the corporate world, there are many reasons to change companies. Even if you don't jump around, there are such good odds the company will dump you.

There is a myth that too many companies on resume make candidates look unstable to employers. That's true if you spend less than two years at nearly every position or you cannot credibly explain the reasons. Having many companies on your resume with reasonable employment tenure has advantages if:

- you had progression of increasing responsibilities and/or acquired marketable experiences and skills.

- you had a career plan you were executing (such as a transition from public school teacher to an Education Sales position at a private corporation.).

- the job change(s) were not in your control (company closure, relocation, merger, or downsizing.).

Why consider staying

- You're still learning new skills and gaining new experiences.

- Your manager is a good leader and mentor.

- You're paid well for what you do.

- There are promotional and growth opportunities.

- Intangibles that meet your current lifestyle, such as company location and benefits.

Why consider leaving

- **Increased Compensation.** Purely from a salary perspective, changing companies, even for the same job, will help you increase your salary and at a faster pace than if you stayed at the same company. Your merit increases do not keep up with the market rates for the same position.

- **Boss from hell.** We already discussed this in an earlier chapter. The short of it is if you have the boss from hell and there is no other position within your current company that you can move into,

LEAVE as soon as you can. The boss from hell not only makes your work life miserable, but also your personal life from all the stress you will experience. Furthermore, the boss from hell will reduce your self-worth and confidence, both important to get ahead of the herd.

- **Blackballed.** Being blackballed is to be labeled within your company, division, or department as a person who should not be promoted. Companies don't use this term, but the result is the same and it does happen. (Just because the term isn't used, does not mean that it doesn't exist.) If this is the case, change companies. You have nothing left at the current one. Sometimes it is obvious you are blackballed. Your manager tells you in so many words and hopefully you learn the reasons. Logically, you should be able to repair whatever your shortcoming is so you do become a viable candidate for advancement in the future. Practically speaking, you are fighting a perception that is very, very difficult to change. That's how human beings work. When people lose confidence in someone, they look only at the mistakes and negative things from that person. And, if by some miracle, you can change someone's confidence in you, it'll take so much time and uncertainty that you'll be better off wiping the slate clean with another company and start off again without the weight and uncertainty attached to your reputation.

- **Troubled company.** Change companies if the company is in trouble and at risk of going out of business. Since I began my career in the early 1980's, I've experienced four recessions. When a company get in trouble, they will lay employees off and they will do this generally in one big slash. Big companies make big job cuts, especially public companies. Public companies prepare for layoffs expenses such things as severance pay along with other write-offs. Executives tell the shareholders and board of directors about the write-off. Executives don't want to go back again and again for more write-offs. Doing so is a reflection that they did not plan well or did not execute the plan well. Both are dangerous career moves (and decreases the stock value). Bottom line, don't delay if there's a hint your company is headed for trouble. Keep your pulse on the market and have feelers out for jobs in case you are laid off. If you are a top performer and/or have good skills and accomplishments, you will do better at getting ahead of any layoffs and downturns. And if you plan it just right, you may be able to take advantage of the company's lay-off package the company "budgeted" for in the write-off (severance, job search service, health benefit, etc.).

- **Diversify your skills.** As you've probably already picked up on throughout this book, I am a big believer in continual learning and improving your skills. That involves getting different experiences. You can't do this if you are stuck in the same job for years. And unless you are changing jobs that have significant difference in work environment, responsibilities, or company functions, you are not learning anything new. You are falling behind your competition in the job marketplace. If you recall one of my golden rules – you should be looking for a change in job and, if necessary, in a different company after 3-5 years in the same job/department.

- **Job Market.** Hiring managers today have no problem with a candidate who has worked at several different companies, provided that the tenure at each company is 2-3 years on the average and each change was a career progression. Despite all the discussion earlier about salary increases by changing companies, you shouldn't change often just to get a small salary increase. There should be more benefits to leaving your current company than just for a small salary increase, such as advancement and the other points made in this section.

- **Geography and Industry.** There are areas of the country (and the world) where companies pay significantly higher. A great case-in-point of both geography and industry opportunities – look at the Silicon Valley/Bay Area in Northern California. "But the cost of living is higher", is generally a how people will response. That's true but it's still worth taking a job there even if it's only for a few years. There are reasons why the cost of living is higher:

  o Everyone is making a whole lot more while there is a limited space to live. So far since the birth of Silicon Valley in the 1970's, salaries have risen and home values have risen (even during the 2007 recession).

  o Leading edge technologies and products provide a hotbed of experiences and skills that can make you more valuable and advance your career.

  o Given the company's growth and continued number of new companies formed, there are tremendous career advancement opportunities.

Squeaky wheels don't get the attention

No, the squeaky wheel (not whiny wheel) DOES get the attention. Be a squeaky wheel in the philosophical sense, not literal sense.

There is a myth that good workers will get noticed and will get the attention and awards, automatically. Recall the advice from my Hewlett-Packard manager who advised me to "toot my horn and voice up" about my accomplishments, career needs and desires. Being Asian himself, he was trying to pass on what he learned and regretted.

The advice wasn't just about Asians or any race or culture at all. The advice is for anyone who has a quiet demeanor or thinks corporate leaders will notice everything you do and shower you with promotion and reward. My HP manager was right on but I did not truly understand when he advised me and I was reluctant to follow his advice. For many years, I never tooted my horn or asked anything from my managers towards improving my career.

Two things held me back:

1. I kept getting exceptional reviews, so I naturally thought things like promotions would come automatically without me asking for them or making a fuss about them. WRONG.

2. Despite the early advice, I found myself being AFRAID and EMBARASSED to ask. The act of asking for something for myself was a lot like not wanting to ask what the price of something is in front of your rich friends. Years later, this quiet "embarrassment" was what my HP manager referred to about be too Asian.

It's OK to ask. And there are professional, witty, clever, proud ways to ask. Best advice is to ask mentors and try out different approaches. At the very least, just be yourself and ask. If you're not sure, ask. Become the squeaky wheel. You want to put the pressure on your superiors by asking them to help you out, give you advice on areas to improve upon, and you should put this burden on your manager. They are stressed by the thought that you need care & feed. Get that action item on their already busy schedule. Managers want to help out their good employees therefore you have to be a good employee. The people that are squeaky are getting attention! Worst case, you'll know where you stand when your manager does nothing with your requests. At that point, you can take the steps to progress your career because your professional future is not with that manager/dept/company.

Jerks don't get ahead

There seems to be enough jerks in corporate hierarchies that the statement must be "false". Jerks do get ahead. It's definitely not 100% of the jerks that get ahead and maybe not even 30%. No one really knows. I just know I've seen enough. Why do you think it happens, even for one jerk?

Let's step back and define a "jerk" in the corporate world. My definitions of a jerk is a person who:

- Is rude to peers and employees at lower levels they interact with; inconsiderate, selfish.

- Kisses up to superiors; brown-noser and shameless yes-person.

- Willing to step on anyone to get whatever they are trying to accomplish; manipulative, no conscience.

- Thinks or acts like they know everything and is better than everyone; arrogant, condensing, bullying.

- Directly and openly criticizes others insensitively.

One reason jerks get ahead is because they actually produce. Jerks are very bright people. They get things done. Conventional thinking (if you read and believe all those management books) would conclude that jerks do not and cannot be tolerated in companies. They create low morale, poor teamwork and the result is lower productivity.

The real world doesn't follow conventional thinking or some research project, however. Jerks don't subscribe to all the conventional thinking. Take the topic of teamwork or, in the jerk's case, lack of it. Even when people don't want to help and in some cases will sabotage what a jerk is trying to do, the jerk knows how to apply pressure or make visible the unwilling employee. They know how to cover their backs and how to cover their tracks. Jerks are the masters of negative politics.

Jerks play off the fact that upper Management is generally only concerned with results, not how the results are achieved. The jerk acts completely different with upper Management, Therefore upper

Management is not aware of the "dead bodies" the jerk leaves among the lower levels. Even if employees complain, I've seen upper Management regularly accept or ignore the complaints because the jerk is producing. And, unless the jerk breaks legal or harassment laws, even HR cannot touch the jerk. And if there was enough noise about a jerk, there's a lot of work involved to build a case to put a jerk on notice. Remember how much work is involved for a manager to reprimand an employee and eventually to fire an employee? The jerks somehow know all this.

Finally, a person can be a jerk because it's just their nature or because they are so driven by some passion that they don't want to spend the energy or effort to be "correct." A perfect example of this was Steve Jobs, the founder and CEO of Apple Computer, in his younger days. I was at Apple towards the later years of Steve's "firing" from Apple and heard many hallway stories about Steve's interpersonal and work "style" (not to mention how well documented it was in the press).

If you haven't heard, Steve was well described as a jerk in the workplace. His behavior and interaction with his employees and partners was such a contradiction to what Silicon Valley was known for during the late 1980's – development of a progressive, humanistic company and management culture. Silicon Valley was anti-IBM, anti-blue suits and white shirts, anti-monarchy, anti-groupthink. Steve was a blend of two cultures. He was the almighty king in a Silicon Valley hippy club. For those employees that were able to withstand Steve's put downs, yelling, bullying, and emotional rollercoaster rides, the remaining employees experienced personal results beyond their imagination. Steve got the most out of the employees. Steve's teams accomplished great things. There was a certain cult influence and leadership Steve imposed. To nearly everyone involved or anyone watching from the outside, Steve was the definition of a jerk. Whatever the case might have been, it all worked for Steve.

Fast-forward to 2010 and we've learned that Steve wasn't a jerk by choice. He was passionately trying to accomplish "insanely" great things, quickly. He did not have time to be polite and courteous. He was also young. Steve happened to be incredibly more brilliant and visionary than 99% of us and we were all getting in his way. So perhaps jerks in some warped righteous manner are good at getting ahead.

What can you learn from a jerk?

- They are not afraid to voice their wants and needs.

- They drive to get things done.

- They are focused on managing up.

- They are extremely persistent.

- They are very confident.

- They are not timid.

- They are very bright and often work hard behind the scenes to learn all they can about all aspects of a project.

How do you work with a jerk?

- Do not work against them. Learn to work with them. They will help you get what you need if it's working towards helping them get what they need done. At the same time, you do not have to go out of your way to do more than you have to.

- Stay professional. Don't make-or take their comments and actions personally, especially when they're criticizing you and/or your work. In many cases, their criticism is valid, so be open-minded because their criticism can lead to a better product/service.

- Don't try to make friends with them. Again, keep it professional.

- Don't arm them with ammunition…give them just enough information.

- You must know as much as they do; more would be better. Stay at an intellectual level with them. They respect smart people.

Good looks do not factor into career growth

Ah, not true. There are tons of studies on this and the results consistently state that good-looking people get ahead more often or have more opportunities to get ahead compared to the not-so-good looking person.

What defines good looks and how does it apply in the corporate world? The corporate world behaves just like society; people favor people they find attractive. A person's looks are a big element of attractiveness. It's not just what you know and whom you know, but it's how you look.

This book is not about a deep discussion about the rights and wrongs about society, sociology, human interaction, and all that influences these elements. The purpose is to make you aware so that you can do something about it. It is difficult to make a universal definition of good looks and attractiveness. Beauty is really in the eye of the beholder. In general, there are shared agreements among people as to what is attractive…and what traits are "challenging":

- Being too short
- Significantly over-weight
- Poor hygiene (body odor)
- Baldness
- Poor dental
- Major facial abnormality

Attractiveness is more than physical looks. Good news is that you can correct many of these challenges. There's even surgery. But you're saying to yourself, "Self, isn't surgery a bit drastic?" It depends on how "challenged" someone is with some of these elements. It's not so far fetched. Many of you already took similar steps – how many of you had orthodontic work to give you perfectly straight teeth. And many of you may also have had teeth whitening done. Good-looking teeth are important, not just in business but in your personal life. When I was 16 years old, our family was poor and we did not have health and dental insurance, so I did not understand why my parents scrapped all they had to pay for orthodontic work for my younger sister but had done nothing for my brothers. When I asked, my mother said, "boys can make a living even with poor looking teeth, but girls rely on getting a good husband". My mother's reasoning may be old fashion but she was right on with the intention and point about the impact of "good looks", especially when faced with economic challenges.

I'd like to touch on the weight "challenge". As a manager, some topics are off limits because of legal reasons, but sometimes it is also due to social reasons. One of those topics had to do with an employee's physical appearance, namely being over-weight. In the corporate world, most jobs do not require someone to meet a physical dimension. There are some insurance penalties being introduced, but in general managers should not discuss weight issues because it is not a job requirement or a condition that directly affects job performance. As a mentoring type of manager, I really wanted to have these discussions with high potential employees because it can hold them back (or better put, other people will have a negative perception of their condition). In one instance, one of my staff members brought up the topic when he shared with me his success with a weight reduction program. I was happy he recognized the possible limitation to his career and was doing something about it.

Other appearance areas you should consider:

- Dress for and look like success. "It is better to be overdressed than underdressed". Dress for the next job/level. Your appearance includes what you wear, how you wear it, and when you wear clothes and accessory. There are several good books and magazines on this topic. I don't mean to appear sexist, but the guys should get some advice about fashion and personal care because guys don't normally learn or seek this information. In addition to getting advice from knowledgeable people (fashion department store clerks at major department stores; girlfriends; well-groomed guy friends), check out magazines like *Men's Health*. Along the same vein, a word for the women – you need to dress and act professionally. Behavior and image for the corporate world is not commonly taught to women as they are growing up. I've lost count of how often my HR Representative told me about complaints they received from employees about how racy and inappropriate employees in my organization were dressed.

- Beyond the physical attractiveness. Beauty is skin deep" meaning what you project also defines how people "see" you. We already discussed projecting a good attitude, good social and interpersonal skills, good communication skills, confidence, intelligence, enthusiasm, etc. People find these traits attractive. Review Chapter: Brand You.

Only bad things can happen to employees of the company being acquired.

Much more true than false.

Acquisition myths:

- "My job cannot be replaced". I have yet to see any job or person in that job that cannot be replaced (some may require a little bit more time, but it happens).

- "We'll be left alone". This may occur for a while. There are situations whereby an acquired company is left completely alone. At

154

some point, usually a year or two after the acquisition is complete, some part or all of the company has changes made.

- "There won't be any changes". Executives generally justify an acquisition on productivity gains. That's a fancy term that means generating additional revenue or new cost reductions through consolidation, relocation, reduction, different process and procedures, closures, or reducing product lines and/or markets. It's not often large investments are made to an acquired company. Either case, there will be changes.

If you are the company being acquired there is a huge likelihood your company will be moved, reduced in size, shutdown, or all of the above. There is rarely anything good that happens to the acquired company.

Don't let the acquiring company executive's rhetoric and nice speeches fool you. The last two quotes in the bullets above are heard often from the acquiring executives. For some reason, either the executives really do have good intentions, they are incompetent, they just want to calm the herd and it's a calculating tactic, or all of the above, but the initial executive communications to the company employees being acquired goes something like this –

"We have the highest respect for your company's culture, performance, and employees; employee especially because that's the main value we purchased XYZ company for. We will evaluate our options, but at this moment we do not see any need to make changes. We plan to let XYZ company run autonomously. We appreciate your continued focus on achieving and maintaining your goals.".

Sounds great doesn't it. Don't for a second believe any of it. As I said, most of the time the acquirer already has plans to get the synergy and productivity from the acquisition. More on that later. Even if the acquirer does have the intention to leave things alone, they will shortly (within a year) take some action because of several "unexpected" developments that include: culture clash, under-performance by acquired company, resistance to change (there will always be some and the change could be as small as some new policy). There are other causes, but you get the picture.

Here's what is going on the other side; from the acquirer's side:

- To begin with, when a company is looking at acquiring another company, there are months of due diligence work in advance of any offer to purchase. Due diligence basically means the acquiring company will plow through all the financial records and any documentation of the acquirer's business. That will include process and procedures, process flow, organization charts, personnel list, patents, sales contracts, supplier contracts, facilities, etc.

- Then, if all looks in order, the acquirer sends teams of people, generally key people from various functions such as Customer Service, Manufacturing, HR, Engineering, and so forth to visit the acquiree's company to see the operations first hand, validate the documentation, and assess the challenges and issues.

- This information is assembled and analyzed to determine a final purchase price and to develop a post-purchase plan. That post-purchase plan will layout what the acquirer plans to do with the acquiree.

Yes, the plan is already in place well before the offer is accepted. Financial models have been developed to look for "productivity" from the acquisition well in advance. As described earlier, "Productivity" is a fancy MBA term to mean reduce, consolidate, or eliminate operations (that includes people). Most of the time, the acquirer is looking for synergy so there are plans to integrate operations wherever possible and that usually means eliminating some duplications. That's productivity!

What can you do if you are in the acquiree company herd?

- Firstly, be helpful to the acquiree's employee and managers if they are trying to understand why your department (and the company as a whole) operates the way it operates. Do NOT defend the way your company is doing what it is doing. That will brand you as being part of the old regime. Understand that the employees from the acquiring company don't know readily what you or the other acquiree company's employee backgrounds are. As far as they are concerned, you are part of the old regime, even if you've only been at the company for a few months. Update your resume but the main thing is to educate the new management team about ALL your background, before your tenure at this current company.

- Secondly, if you have special knowledge about a task or something critical to the department, don't keep it a secret thinking it'll save your job. Most acquiring managers are looking to keep the brightest and smartest employees. In fact, an acquisition is a great time to let go poor performing employees in the acquirer company! Given how difficult it is to fire poor performers, one of the safest times to do it is during the integration after an acquisition. The acquiring company actually will budget in the model for write-offs, such as facility closures and layoffs.

- Lastly, get your resume out on the street just to be safe. It's better to get a job while you are employed than when you are laid off. Hiring managers understand smart candidates want to get ahead of changes. It's more difficult to explain how special you are when you are among an entire group of people laid off.

There's a good chance I'll be laid off in my career

A very good chance. For the foreseeable future, the threat of layoffs is the new normal.

A layoff has many names: reduction, streamlining, downsizing, rightsizing, process re-engineering, and eliminating redundancy. When economic times are good, companies don't have layoffs except when there is an acquisition or merger. When times are tough, like they are these days, companies will have layoffs sooner rather than later in order to set up for the long term, even when their business is doing alright. This is especially true with public corporations. They cut expenses early and in big chunks to appease the Wall Street community. Wall Street will tolerate a major expense reduction. The size of the reduction is not too important. What Wall Street hates (and will punish the corporation's stock price for) is when there are several reductions.

Companies legitimately use layoffs to reduce expenses. Sometimes companies have layoffs in anticipation of continued difficult business conditions ahead. Layoffs are also a great time for managers to eliminate poor performing employees, even if they don't have an expense reduction reason. The main reason is that to fire an employee for poor performance reasons is difficult, involves a lot of work, and carries a lot of legal risk and expense to the company. Here are some insights and tips:

Get early warning. Keep a pulse with your internal networks (IT, facilities, Finance departments). They would be one of the first to know if the company is looking at making or becoming an acquisition. They would also know early on if there will be an expense reduction activity like a layoff.

Stronger signs of trouble. Keep aware of the company's performance (sales and expenses) to budget and what the sales forecast is for the company's remaining fiscal year. A typical pattern when there are signs of trouble will be an executive edict to freeze hiring that can include no headcount requisitions to back fill for attrition. Then there will be an executive edict to cut expenses by some percentage for the remaining fiscal year. Note that even in good economic times, a company can under-perform in terms of hitting its financial goals, which can lead to cost-cutting measures.

Don't sit there in fantasyland thinking nothing is going to happen. Management CANNOT tell employees anything about plans, next steps, or speculations. I've seen so many employees get hung up and angry because they believe companies should treat them like "family members" and be "honest" about what is going to happen. DREAM ON! Public companies are prohibited by SEC rules, because the news could affect stock transactions. Even private companies not constrained by SEC rules won't risk revealing internal performance information and plans to employees to minimize spooking vendors and customers and tipping information to competitors. Also, if the employer told the employees about upcoming layoffs then the employees would start looking for new jobs outside the company. The company knows that the A-players would be the most likely to find new jobs and the poor performing employees will stay. So, to keep the A-players and get rid of the poor performers, the company must keep upcoming layoffs a secret.

Rumors are usually true. I'm not talking about gossip. I'm talking about hallway rumors of major company actions. I don't have any research to cite (and not sure how you would structure this sort of research), but my experience has been that rumors about major company actions are 80-90% true. I have personally been at five companies that have had at least one layoff or an acquisition or had a major facilities move or had a major downturn in business. Just about every layoff, expense reduction, hiring freeze, move to a new location, facility shutdown, or acquisition/merger rumor came true. And I acted on several. The best one was when I worked at a Sun Microsystem division in Northern California. There was a rumor that the division was moving all 2,000 positions to Boulder, Colorado. My family was not interested in moving so, given the lead-time I gained, I landed another positions. The plus was that the position was a promotion for me.

You should always keep a pulse on the job market, even if you don't need a job. I don't mean to throw your resume out on the street or contact recruiters. I'm suggesting that you simply monitor the job market. You should have your resume updated and posted on some job sites and recruiters. You do not have to be actively looking all the time. It can be distracting to hear about job opportunities when you are doing well at one. Occasionally it is good to know what your position is worth or maybe, just maybe, that dream job might surface. You should be familiar with possible companies in your area you can target if need be.

There is nothing wrong with you being prepared. Don't feel like you are being disloyal to your company. It's business. Your company (and Management) is also making plans and contingencies that affect employee resources and they are not going to tell you. The corporate world is a mercenary environment – each party's foremost priority is their own well-being and both sides will go where the money is. Corporations need to make their goals. Employees (acting like Employee, Inc.) need to make their personal goals. Neither party has a goal to "be loyal." Loyalty is an outdated concept. Loyalty implies that either party owes the other something for past employer-employee business dealings. Any loyalty is toward delivering the services being rendered. Corporations pay you for services and, in return, you should deliver them 110% results. The extra 10% is your investment towards advancement, merit increases, bonuses, etc. Beyond what you are paid to do and any legal obligations, such as non-disclosures and non-compete agreements, the company owes you nothing else, you owe the company nothing else, and neither party should expect any entitlement.

Human Resources is NOT the individual contributor's friend

With respect to general benefits and company policies, such as questions about hiring practices or how the health plan works, and legal policies, such as sexual harassment, then yes, they are on your side. For these topics, they are on every employee's side, regardless of rank. But when it comes to interpersonal issues you have with management or a beef you have with the company culture, make no mistake, that friendly HR representative in your corporation is NOT on the individual contributor's side. HR serves management. HR meets with management daily. HR is involved WITH management in all strategic planning, company's annual organization reviews, staff planning, succession planning, etc.

I know what you are thinking – "but Tony, my company has an open culture. It's a family. There is a lot of integrity. Blah blah blah." Pleeeease, do NOT buy into all the company culture and vision stuff. I hate to burst your naïve bubble, but these fluffy ideals are at best short-lived, even if they do actually exist in some companies; and they mostly exist only in small companies. As soon as the company grows larger, it is nearly impossible for the culture to sustain itself. Sorry for digressing, but the point I'm trying to help you to understand is that employees with (non-illegal) complaints about the management and company should NOT go running to their HR Representative with their grievances. The HR person will share this with your management. They are not lawyers and are not obligated by some attorney/physician-client privilege rule. There is no confidentiality clause involved here. At best, your manager will treat it as being trivial. At worst, your image is tarnished forever among people who are in a position to promote you or influence a promotion. I've seen and experienced this, unfortunately, several times early in my career. When I moved into management, I was horrified to see the "other side", yet I appreciated receiving the insight into who the "complaining" employees were and what they complained about.

Key Actions Checklist

☐ Register onto www.moooveahead.com to get supplemental information and advice from articles, links, tips, and blogs.

☐ Final quote from one of my favorite movies, Star Wars: Episode 4 (the first one) to all of you in how you approach your professional career: "Do or do not, there is no *try*" ~ Yoda

☐ Stay humble. Don't forget the little people when you move ahead in the corporate herd.

☐ Give back. When you move ahead of the herd, help others. Give to charities. Mentor others trying to get ahead of the herd. You'll receive more than what you're giving, trust me. This book is my way of walking the talk. I wrote this book to help young people and to help charities – I will donate all sales proceeds to charities. My gratification comes from your career success and from helping charities help others.

About the Author

Tony Wong has spent 27 years in corporate America starting out as a young cow in the herd and eventually mooove towards the front of the herd in Director level positions at several Fortune 125 companies. The chronological list of companies include NCR, Hewlett-Packard, Apple Computer, Sun Microsystems, Motorola/Printrak, Gateway Computer, Black & Decker, Firmgreen, and Federal Signal Technologies.

All along Tony was just consumed with earning a living and providing for his family, like most people who are working in some organization. Never did he take notice of all the insight he learned....until a couple of years ago when circumstances allowed him to realize most people working in the corporate world do not or have not learned what it takes to mooove ahead, soooner. Some people don't have guidance. Some people are too busy to notice. Moreover, the information is not readily available (I'm learning firsthand it's not easy to write a book and now I can see why there hasn't been more successful corporate mooovers documenting their operational tips and wisdom).

Tony's goal for the book and related revenue is to donate every penny to charities he will be partnering with. Follow him on Twitter (Mooovers), Facebook (Moooveahead), and email (moooveahead@yahoo.com), for information about upcoming website/blog, seminars, charities, and additional insights and tips to help people Mooove Ahead of the (corporate) Herd, soooner!